Timeless Wisdom on Current Issues

Chaitanya Charan Das

Vedic Oasis for Inspiration, Culture and Education (VOICE),
S.No.50, Katraj Kondhwa Bypass,
Opposite to Shatrunjay Temple, Pune-411 048.
Phone: +91-86050-36000
Email: voicebooks@voicepune.com

VOICE invites readers interested in this book to correspond at the following address:

Sales Manager:
Krishnakishore das
A-102, Bharati Vihar, Katraj, Pune – 411 046
Phone: +91-98224-51260
Email: krishnakishoredas@gmail.com

First Printing: 28th Aug 2013, 1000 copies

Dedicated to

HDG AC Bhaktivedanta Swami Prabhupada,

the founder-acharya of ISKCON,

Who expertly explained the relevance, indeed the necessity, of Vedic wisdom for contemporary times

&

To all those who wish to empower themselves with time-honored wisdom

Contents

Introduction

"It is already becoming clear that a chapter which had a Western beginning will have to have an Indian ending if it is not to end in the self-destruction of the human race. At this supremely dangerous moment in history, the only way of salvation for mankind is the Indian way."

- British historian Dr Arnold Toynbee

"I am convinced that India could become once again the cradle of a new school of thought that may significantly influence the fate of the globe during the third millennium. Perhaps the contribution of India to nuclear power technology and space science will turn out to be irrelevant, but the contributions toward a new ethical foundation could be turning the wheel of history in the proper (balanced) way."

- Nobel Laureate Dr Richard Ernst

The relevance and coherence of Vedic wisdom was what attracted me to it over fifteen years ago in 1996 – and it continues to fascinate me even today.

As an Indian born and brought up in a pious culture, I had gone for pilgrimages with my relatives and had memorized many verses of the Bhagavad-gita for shloka recitation contests. But I had never found all this relevant to my needs, interests and concerns as a young, educated and scientifically-minded Indian.

Yet when I met Hare Krishna devotees, and studied the writings of

Srila Prabhupada and his followers, I was stunned to see how the insights they shared were far more relevant than anything I had come across till then. Those insights helped me see my own life as well as the world around me in a fresh, meaningful and purposeful light.

As I started investigating Vedic wisdom and its relevance, I was amazed to find that thousands, even millions, all over the world were discovering it to be intellectually fulfilling and spiritually empowering. Yoga, karma, and mantra – these words had not just become an integral part of English vocabulary but were also the bedrocks of a coherent and cogent worldview that has the potential to bring balance and harmony to our current world.

Thus began an intellectual and spiritual exploration of Vedic wisdom that led me to read hundreds of books. So exciting and fulfilling were my findings that I felt inspired to share them through speaking and writing – and to make sharing those findings my life mission.

This book is a distilled compilation of some of those findings. It is an edited anthology of the articles that I have written as a part of the Vedic Observer column in ISKCON's official magazine, Back to Godhead. This column aims to focus the spotlight of Vedic wisdom on current issues and outline spiritual solutions to contemporary problems.

I have divided this book's fourteen articles into four sections. The first section "Society" addresses social issues such as sexual violence, disruption of the ecology and the failed promises of materialism. The second section "Science" deals with developments in the scientific world like the discovery of the God particle and the claimed synthesis of artificial life. It also responds to the common fallacy of equating science, the open-minded search for knowledge of the natural world, with scientism, the narrow-minded belief system that arrogates to science a monopoly on human knowledge. The third section "Religion" addresses the emerging trend of SBNR (spiritual but not religious), the delicate issue of religious conversions, the abortive attempt in Russia to brand the Gita as extremist, and the relevance of ancient texts like the Ramayana and traditional festivals like Janmashtami. The last section "The Individual" outlines how spiritual wisdom can empower us to face the anti-spiritual currents of the current age as well as reversals such as the loss of loved ones and the onslaught of life-threatening diseases.

I hope that you will find these glimpses into the relevance of timeless Vedic wisdom that I have gleaned from my many spiritual teachers enlightening and empowering.

Chaitanya Charan Das
Editor, Back to Godhead
Member, Shastric Advisory Council

Society

Delhi gang-rape and the modern Shurapanakha

"The sexual exposure we face is unparalleled in the history of mankind... Because pornography and sex have such a forceful pull on us, if left unchecked our society will erode before our very eyes. We will have millions of people who have sexual addictions."

-*'Treating Pornography Addiction'* by Dr. Kevin B. Skinner

The horrifying gang-rape of a young physiotherapy student in a private bus in Delhi in December 2012 sparked outrage across the country. The innocuous-seeming circumstances in which the rape occurred, the bloodcurdling brutality of the perpetrators, the ineptitude of the police and the seeming insensitivity of the Prime Minister have all added fuel to the fire.

Before addressing this issue, I offer my sincere prayers for the departed soul of the victim and my heartfelt condolences to her bereaved and traumatized family. Gita wisdom teaches us that all of us are relatives, connected in God's all-encompassing family. So we are all together in getting over this tragedy.

The Delhi horror underscores undeniably that our female citizens absolutely require much better security. We need a more vigilant police force, prompter help-lines, and stronger and swifter punishments for sexual assaulters.

Yet will better security be enough? Might our society be suffering from a more deep-rooted malaise of which this gruesome rape is an intolerably stinking symptom? After all, the news periodically reports incidents of scary sexual violence. School-teacher extracting sexual favors from a girl-student in the classroom; father having incest with his daughter in the presence of his son; mother and daughter hacking to death a man with whom both had an affair – these are the headlines from just a week's news.

Surely something is terribly wrong in our society, but what is it?

The topic of sexual assault is complex; sociologists include anger, power and sadism among its causes. Here, I will focus on one important aspect largely overlooked by the media but illumined by Vedic wisdom.

The little-discussed Shurapanakha factor

In the Vedic tradition, the demon Ravana, the villain of the Ramayana, is the emblem of lust. Lust so dominated Ravana that he abducted beautiful women wherever he found them and forced them to join his harem. He even raped a relative, the celestial nymph Rambha, who was married to his nephew. Thereafter he was cursed to die if he raped any women. So, when he abducted Sita for enjoying her sexually, he threatened to kill and eat her if she didn't voluntarily comply. Thus, for the sake of gratifying his sexual appetite he had a proclivity to rape and to commit other types of horrible violence against women. He finally met his just end when Lord Rama administered capital punishment.

We all know of Ravana's perversity, but a crucial detail underlying his perversity is less known. The Ramayana describes that though thoughts of possessing Sita initially allured Ravana, he gave up his evil intentions when he was told about the unmatchable power of Rama. However, when his malicious sister Shurapanakha incited him by describing Sita's beauty explicitly and provocatively, he lost all sense and courted self-destruction. Shurapanakha had her own scores to settle and she used Ravana as her pawn by inciting him.

The Ramayana, in addition to being an ancient history, features characters who are prototypes for perennial themes. In our current context, Ravana obviously symbolizes sexual perverts like the Delhi rapists. What does Shurapanakha symbolize? She symbolizes the forces that incite people sexually and make them behave in Ravana-like ways.

The modern Shurapanakha

Today's primary sexual inciter, the modern Shurapanakha, is the commercial world that uses sex to sell its products. The commercial world knows that sex is the best sales tool because nothing catches people's attention and triggers their imagination as much as sex. So it exploits sex as its ubiquitous marketer and fills our culture with sexually provocative images.

This commercial exploitation of sex is all the more flagrant in the entertainment industry, especially Hollywood and Bollywood, where sex is arguably the most glamorized product on sale. And the modern Shurapanakha is at its blatant worst as the pornography industry, where sex, even brutal sex, is the only product on sale. Commercial porn websites, magazines, books, videos, DVDs, cable television, etc. comprise one of the most lucrative global industries. In the United States alone, porn revenue is larger than the combined revenues of all professional football, baseball and basketball franchises.

Due to this massive commercial exploitation, sex is thrust upon us from all directions – TV, theaters, internet, magazines and billboards. Practically wherever we look, sexually provocative images are pushed into our eyes. The way human culture has become sexualized in the last several decades has no precedent in world history.

The Deadly Consequence of Liberalization

The modern Shurapanakha incites in a much more insidious way than the Ramayana Shurapanakha. It fools us into believing that becoming its pawn, that is, becoming sexually incited, is a sign of sexual liberalization. To understand how such liberalization can entrap us, let's first look at the rationale for sexual restraint.

The Bhagavad-gita (07.10) offers us insight into the sanctity of sex: when performed within the precincts of dharma, it offers us an opportunity to experience the divine. Sex enables us to become co-creators with God in bringing new life into the world.

At the same time, Gita wisdom cautions us that when sex is divorced from this divine perspective and purpose, it becomes motivated by a deadly force that impels people into perversity. In the Bhagavad-gita (03.36), Arjuna asks Krishna: what makes people act sinfully, even against their will? This eternally relevant question is presently resonant. Krishna answers (Gita 03.37) that the evil inner impeller is lust which is the all-devouring sinful enemy of the world. Then he outlines how a philosophically informed and devotionally centered culture empowers us to keep lust under control.

Traditionally, the sexual force was regulated by the sacred inviolable covenant of marriage. The modern Shurapanakha has persuaded us that this covenant is too regressive and repressive, and so we need to liberate ourselves from it. Being thus taken in, we approve the release of this force from within the fence of covenant each time we delight in sexually explicit imagery, language and music.

However, lust once released can rapidly veer out of control. The

Bhagavad-gita (03.39) states that lust is like an insatiable fire. Indulgence acts as the fuel that aggravates the fire. So, when we release the force of lust a bit through indulgence, it becomes that much stronger and demands more release through greater indulgence. When we accede, it becomes stronger still and demands still greater release, thereby trapping us. What we might have thought of as unconscionable before we released lust may over time become acceptable, then enjoyable and finally irresistible. This is how the modern Shurapanakha makes many people into sexual perverts.

The English satirist Alexander Pope in his *An Essay on Man* echoes how vice – the modern Shurapanakha in our context – inverts our sensibilities:

Vice is a monster of so frightful mien

As to be hated needs but to be seen

Yet seen too oft, familiar with her face,

We first endure, then pity, then embrace.

- Alexander Pope

Understanding this insidious nature of lust can help us see the link between the generic commercial exploitation of sex and this specific ghastly sexual assault: the force that we release in the name of liberalization is the same force that in a later stage impels such fiendish crimes.

By no means is this metaphorical analysis of lust as a monster meant to shift the blame away from the rapists; they are responsible for letting the monster pervert them. The purpose of this analysis is to point out that their barbarism is not an anomaly that can be rectified just by stronger legal measures; it is a detestable but natural consequence of the feverish sexualization that has permeated our culture.

How the unconscionable can become the real

We may doubt: "Most commercial depictions of sex in the media portray romantic and consensual sex. How can that lead to such perversity?"

Not all commercial sexual depictions are consensual; the reprehensible glamorization of violent sex in extreme forms of pornography is a significant exception. But even if we set aside this exception, the fact remains that the commercial depiction of sex is designed to trigger lust. And once this hideous monster is aroused, it can become blind to the difference between sanctified sex and profane sex. It can become blinder still so as to see no difference between consensual sex and forcible sex. And at its blindest, it can no longer distinguish between sex alone and sex mixed with violence, torture, maiming, and murder. Due to this blinding nature of lust, the Bhagavad-gita cautions us that it is "the destroyer of knowledge and self-realization" (Gita 3.41) and is "our eternal enemy" (Gita 3.39).

Those who give a free rein to this monster become the modern Ravanas. In fact, they end up becoming worse than the Ramayana Ravana; the barbarous violence of the Delhi rapists far exceeded what Ravana did to anyone. These perverts need to be swiftly and visibly meted out the necessary severe punishment, as was done by Lord Rama to Ravana.

But we also need to remember that the Shurapanakha which incited them is inciting everyone, including us too. Of course, the savagery of the Delhi rapists is unthinkable for any civilized person. Yet, appalling as all incidents of sexual violence are, they happen frequently not just in India but all over the world. So, it would surely be naïve and simplistic to demonize these perpetrators alone and give a clean chit to everyone else, including ourselves.

Perhaps this revolting gang-rape is the jolt necessary to drive home the reality that self-serving interests are manipulating us. They are exploiting our sexuality to fill their bank accounts while propelling us on a self-destructive track of increasingly aggressive lust. Liberalization is the ploy that is deceiving us to willingly, even eagerly, play into the hands of the modern Shurapanakha.

If we don't curb the modern Shurapanakha, then just as the knowledge of Rama's power couldn't deter the lust-maddened Ravana, the knowledge of severe legal punishments won't deter the modern lust-maddened Ravanas.

The fetish for political correctness

Today speaking against sexual liberalization is widely considered politically incorrect. Severe political backlash silences those who have the audacity to suggest that anything might be wrong with liberalization.

Pertinently, the Ramayana depicts the results of a fetish for political correctness. Soon after Ravana played into the hands of Shurapanakha and abducted Sita, he started witnessing the consequences of his suicidal folly: Hanuman with his tail-blazing and trail-blazing exploits reduced nearly half of Lanka to ashes.

The distraught Ravana called an emergency meeting of his ministers. In that council, saying that the demon-king had erred in abducting Sita was politically incorrect. So his bootlicking ministers just recommended better security measures for Lanka as the solution. Hardly anyone dared to go against the canon of political correctness. The only vocal politically incorrect dissident was Vibhishana; he boldly and firmly urged Ravana to give up his lust for Sita and return her to Rama.

Unfortunately, Ravana was too possessed by the monster of lust to even consider this sound advice. He curtly silenced Vibhishana's dissenting voice and thereby sealed his own pact with death.

Despite the differences between this Ramayana situation and the gang-rape aftermath, the central point of the parallel is valid and vital: will we choose political correctness or corrective reform?

Towards a liberalizing respiritualization

If we choose reform, then each one of us can make a tangible contribution. All of us have the power to stop being puppets of the modern Shurapanakha; we can individually rebel against the rabid sexualization of our culture. Each time we dress, each time we look at others, each time we respond to sexually overt or covert language, we have the power to make a statement: "I will no longer be a pawn in the hands of those who exploit my sexuality." Every such statement is not just a statement; it is also a contribution to the progressive curing of the sexual fever that is pandemic in our culture.

To accelerate this healing, Gita wisdom offers us an intellectual foundation and a practical pathway. It helps us understand that we are not our bodies, but are eternal souls. We are beloved parts of Krishna, who is our all-attractive all-loving Lord. Our infatuation with sex is a distorted reflection of our original love for him. By redirecting our love towards him, we can relish a deep inner happiness that helps us regulate and transcend sexual craving.

And the process of devotional service offers us a practical means for redirecting our love towards Krishna. Devotional culture naturally focuses on Krishna and minimizes all distractions. That's why in such a culture neither men nor women highlight or aggravate their sexuality. Instead, both focus on developing their latent spirituality. We see each other not as potential sex objects but as spiritual beings, as fellow travelers on an epic devotional voyage back to Krishna. Such a vision helps us strive undistractedly for inner fulfillment. The more we become spiritually fulfilled, the more we become liberated from the constant craving for sex. When sexual fantasies no longer dissipate our mental energy, we become free to fully use our abilities and resources for our own and others' holistic well-being. That is real liberalization indeed.

Decreasing the sexualization of our culture and participating in its re-spiritualization – that is the twofold solution to the grave problem of sexual violence.

****

Question: Doesn't blaming the culture for the Delhi gang-rape mean that we shift the blame away from the criminals?

Answer: No, not at all. It just means that we look at all the relevant causes. Let's understand this with the analogy of arson.

Suppose our city is ravaged repeatedly by conflagrations set off by arson. To counter the menace, we would punish the arsonists strongly and improve the firefighting services. Additionally, we would investigate an underlying cause: are the city buildings made of inflammable stuff?

Similarly, to counter the fire of sexual violence, we absolutely need to punish the criminals swiftly and severely, and to provide better security for women. Additionally, we need to investigate an underlying cause. As all actions start with thoughts – the stuff of the mind, we need to check whether people's thoughts are made of sexually inflammable stuff.

The answer is a resounding yes; vested interests have widely sexualized our culture so as to exploit us commercially.

What is the result of exposure to sexually provocative material? Arson in the mind and arson in the world. Gita wisdom offers pertinent insights. The Bhagavad-gita (03.39) compares lust, the dark force that drives most people towards sex and sexual violence, to a fire. The Gita's next verse (03.40) pinpoints the location of lust to be the mind of the beholder – and not the beholden object – thereby exposing the perversity of blaming the victim for any sexual assault. And its next verse (03.41) recommends regulating one's sensual input as a necessary first step for controlling lust.

Why?

The mind functions according to the well-known GIGO (garbage in, garbage out) principle. In fact, the mind can even aggravate and pervert the ingested garbage before excreting it. The Bhagavad-gita (02.62) explains that lust when frustrated transmogrifies into wrath. Metaphorically, Gita wisdom calls wrath the younger brother of lust (*kamanuja*). External lust-provoking stimuli fill the mind with sexually inflammable stuff. When those whose minds are thus inflammable come across some opportunity for indulgence, that opportunity triggers the fire of desire inside them. This fire can burn down their intelligence and conscience, and make them into sexual perverts who can stoop to the level of using bloodcurdling violence to fulfill their evil desires. That's how even the input of romantic and consensual sex that our sensibilities consider harmless, can by the volatile combustion of lust and wrath, emerge as the output of forcible and brutal sexual violence that our sensibilities condemn as horrendous.

If we don't address this underlying cause, the consequences will be ominous as Dr Kevin B Skinner points out in *Treating Pornography Addiction*, "We will have an epidemic of incredible proportions with no way of turning back. Our social system has allowed greed and money to destroy the lives of men, women, and their children. Families are being destroyed, while those who produce such media are reaping the financial benefits."

To counter this looming disaster effectively, we need to decrease the public depiction of provocative material. By thus changing the stuff that fills our culture externally, we can help make the stuff that fills people's minds less sexually inflammable.

The Save Yamuna Campaign

Where Environmental Activism and Devotional Service Unite

Few topographical changes are as tragic as the death of a river. Thousands of years ago, the disappearance of the Sarasvati River reduced a fertile and flourishing tract of land in Northwestern India to the barren expanse now known as the Thar Desert. Today the Yamuna River, one of the largest water-resources in India, faces the same fate; indeed, the United Nations has already declared the Yamuna a dead river[1], indicating that it is no longer capable of sustaining human, animal or plant life.

But, fortunately, all is not lost; the death of the Sarasvati River was caused by natural forces that were irresistible and irreversible, whereas the present damage to the Yamuna River is caused by human influences that are resistible and reversible. And there's reason to hope for a beneficial change in the human influences. Environmentalists value the Yamuna as a precious natural resource, and devotees of Lord Krishna honor her as an indispensable devotional treasure in whose water Krishna played. Therefore, the campaign to save the Yamuna has the potential to unite environmentalists and devotees on a common platform, possibly opening a new chapter for both.

The disheartening implications of the Yamuna crisis and the heartening networking of environmental and devotional groups in the campaign to save it have been analyzed by Professor Dr. David Haberman, Department Chair, Religious Studies, Indiana University,

---

[1]http://www.unhabitat.org/content.asp?typeid=19&catid=460&id=2170
I am indebted to Gautam Saha for providing this as well as several other references in this article.

Bloomington in his book: *River of Love in the Age of Pollution: The Yamuna River of Northern India.*

The Death of a River

Devotees see the river Yamuna not just as a body of water but also as an eternal spiritual goddess who facilitates and participates in Lord Krishna's pastimes when He comes to the material world. *Shrimad-Bhagavatam* details many of the pastimes that Lord Krishna performed in her waters as well as on her banks. In particular, the *Bhagavatam's* Tenth Canto contains many descriptions of Yamuna's beauty, for instance: "The cowherd boys let the cows drink the clear, cool and wholesome water of the Yamuna. O King Parikshit, the cowherd boys also themselves drank that sweet water to their full satisfaction." (10.23.37)

For devotee-pilgrims, who have been visiting Vrindavana for centuries, the flowing Yamuna has flooded the mind with remembrances of the Lord. She is a merciful mother who bestows blessings of devotional service and a potent purifier who cleanses the heart of contamination. Shrila Rupa Gosvami charmingly depicts this multi-faceted glory of the Yamuna in his *Stava-mala:* "Sprinkling a single drop of her water on oneself destroys the reaction of the most heinous crimes. She increases the flow of confidential devotional service (*raganuga-bhakti*) for Nandanananda within one's heart and blesses everyone who simply desires to reside on her banks. May Yamuna-devi, the daughter of Surya-deva, always purify me." Shrila Prabhupada likewise stresses the importance of the Yamuna in his purport to *Shrimad-Bhagavatam* (6.5.28): "Bathe in the Yamuna, chant the Hare Krishna mantra, and then become perfect and return back to Godhead."

An article in the New Delhi *Hindustan Times* (June 23, 2010) reported the agonizing experience of a sixty-two-year-old man who had a lifelong habit of starting every day with a bath in the Yamuna, in keeping with a tradition that extends far back into history. He had been forced to discontinue this traditional dip "because for a hundred-kilometer stretch between Delhi and Saharanpur district in western Uttar Pradesh, the Yamuna has disappeared. Only miles and miles of sand remain." A photo accompanying the article showed the empty riverbed being used as a roadway for trucks. For this man "who now bathes at home, the drying of the river he once worshiped is a personal tragedy. 'The death of the Yamuna here is like a disaster in my life,' he said in a choking voice."

What Has Caused the Yamuna Crisis?

The Yamuna crisis is caused by two primary factors: depletion and pollution.

1. **Depletion:**

    According to Government of India statistics, the Yamuna River provides water to a massive hinterland of 366,223 kilometers in several states of Northern India. The Yamuna, like many other Indian rivers, gets depleted in the non-monsoon season. But what brings matters to the tipping point of crisis is the indiscriminate and excessive human intervention in its flow. Along the Yamuna's long path, multiple barrages have been constructed that divide it during the non-monsoon season into four distinct segments. At these barrages, almost ninety-seven percent of the water is diverted to local towns and farmlands, with only a small trickle left to continue downstream. In each case this trickle dries up within a few kilometers, after which the riverbed turns into dry land. One mortifyingly large dry patch is the hundred-kilometer stretch between Saharanpur and Delhi already mentioned.

2.   Pollution:

If the river gets depleted to the point of drying out, then how does it continue on?

With polluted water.

It gets refilled with town runoffs and effluents, farm discharges, and industrial effluents, and incidental ground water. Moreover, all the towns and villages adjoining the Yamuna, including the national capital Delhi, dump partly treated or untreated sewage into the river, resulting in high contamination levels.

To be considered safe for human consumption, water must have a BOD (biological oxygen demand – in milligrams per liter) not exceeding 3. But the BOD of the Yamuna water has been seen to be about 51 during the monsoons and as high as 103 during the non-monsoon periods. Additionally, lead and other heavy metals like iron and zinc together with pesticides, arsenic, and NDM 1 (a gene present in bacteria that live in water – this gene makes the bacteria immune to all known antibiotics) are also present in the water in quantities way beyond the maximum acceptable limits.

The magnitude of this depletion-cum-pollution is so

alarming that the Central Pollution Control Board of the Government of India has declared that there is not a drop of natural river water in the Yamuna at Vrindavana[2].

Devotional Dynamism

How can devotees reconcile their conception of Yamuna as an eternal goddess with the perception of Yamuna as a dying river, depleted and polluted?

The reconciliation comes by understanding how and why the divine manifests itself in the material realm. Let's consider the example of a Deity. The all-powerful Lord Krishna manifests Himself in Deity form to give us opportunities to remember and serve Him. Yet, when ignorant or malevolent people under the grip of iconophobia threaten to harm the Deity, devotees don't rest apathetically on the presumption that nobody can harm Krishna; they rise proactively with the conviction that it is their responsibility to protect the Deity. They see this situation of protecting the deity form of the Lord as an exceptional service-opportunity provided by the Lord, who is always their protector. In fact, the devotees in medieval India who exhibited courage and ingenuity in their attempts to "rescue" the Deities of Vrindavana from fanatical Muslim emperors like Aurangzeb are an inspiration for all generations of devotees.

Today a similar "rescue" operation is needed for the Yamuna River. On a spiritual level the goddess Yamuna is beyond being harmed by any material phenomena. But on a material level the river is being polluted, and devotees see the situation as an exceptional service-opportunity to protect the mother-goddess who has till now been protecting and nourishing them.

---

[2]http://www.cpcb.nic.in/newsitems/11.pdf

What Needs to Be Done?

There are several practical and feasible measures that if implemented can minimize and even reverse the crisis. Let's look at one measure for countering each of the two factors that have caused the crisis:

1. **Depletion** can be countered by implementing policies for sustainable water resources management. An Allahabad High Court order (in response to PIL no. 4003 of 25 January 2011), in the case of *Ganga Pollution vs. The State of Uttar Pradesh*, states, "Not more than fifty percent of the water should be drawn from the river at any given place." If this order is extended to the Yamuna, then depletion will be tackled at its roots.

2. **Pollution** can be countered by redirecting the pollutants that are presently being dumped into the Yamuna. Partially or fully treated town effluent, though deleterious to river water, can serve as a major source of water and nutrients for farmlands. If a canal is constructed to divert most of Delhi's sewage into the Agra canal, then the Yamuna can be saved from pollution and Agra can be provided with water for irrigation. A similar strategy for redirecting the effluents from Kolkata that were previously being dumped into the Hooghly has already been successfully implemented.

There are many other measures that need to be adopted, but these two examples underscore what will be needed to implement any major measure: political will.

What Can We Do?

In a democratic country, political will can be significantly, even decisively, influenced by mass mobilization. It is here that the alliance of environmentalists and devotees can play a vital, even critical, role. In fact, the alliance is already there, as explained by Dr Haberman,-: "As devotional service to Yamuna Maiya, educational programs have been launched, clean-up days have been scheduled, boatmen have been organized and enlisted in restorative work, and PILs have been filed in the courts, resulting in sewage treatment plants being built, polluting industry shut down, and minimum flows established for river health. Such work – which already exists and is enacted as loving service to Yamuna-devi herself – demonstrates the great potential for a more robust and effective alliance between environmental scientists and policy makers and members of religious communities. This work represents an initial trickle that may just turn into a mighty river of restorative action."

Among the several religious-spiritual forums joining hands in this effort to save the Yamuna, Braj Raj Sharan Swami and his team from 'Maan Mandir' in Barsana have been a pivotal driving force in recent efforts to increase public awareness.

ISKCON being a global organization has played its part. It has initiated and executed major public awareness drives in its centers all over the world including America, Europe, Russia and, of course, India. The Executive Committee of ISKCON's highest administrative body, the Governing Body Commission, has issued a statement urging ISKCON devotees to take an active role and has given the following broad suggestions of what can be done:

All ISKCON temples, congregations, *yatras,* and devotees please:

1. Include Yamuna Maharani in your daily prayers.

2. Explain the spiritual importance of Shri Yamuna Maharani to others.

3. Organize special kirtans or dedicate existing kirtans to the Yamuna cause.

4. Organize special programs or dedicate existing programs to the Yamuna cause.

5. Explain the environmental issues to others, especially working through the relevant ISKCON ministries that deal with the environment.

6. Create worldwide campaigns.

7. Encourage and assist in petitions to accomplish the aforementioned purposes.

8. Effectively use internal media (Back to Godhead, etc.) and external media (newspapers, television, etc.).

9. Spread this cause all over the world through print media, audio-video media, SMS, Internet (dandavats.com, desiretree.com, etc.), and social media (Facebook, etc.).

The Save Yamuna campaign offers a perfect opportunity for devotional service, especially for those devotees who have long had an environmentalist lying dormant inside them. And as Lord Krishna assures Arjuna in the *Bhagavad-gita* (11.33), if we do our part in His plan, Krishna empowers us to do extraordinary things and make miracles happen. As the Yamuna crisis unfolds, the confluence of ecological and devotional concerns may well be setting the stage for miracles to happen.

The American Paradox and the Indian Parable

"The American Paradox – Spiritual Hunger in an Age of Plenty" by David G Myers is one among the several books that use telling facts and revealing statistics to examine the reality behind the globally-glamorized American dream of the happy life through wealth and sensual enjoyment.

Since 1960,

- The divorce rate has doubled.

- The teen suicide rate has tripled.

- The recorded violent crime rate has quadrupled.

- The prison population has quintupled.

- The percentage of babies born to unmarried parents has sextupled.

- Cohabitation (a predictor of future divorce) has increased sevenfold.

- Depression has soared—to ten times the pre–World War II level.

Has the American dream turned out to be a masked nightmare? What went wrong?

For devotees of Lord Krishna, this sad situation is a demonstration of Krishna's teachings in the Bhagavad-gita wherein he declares in 5.22 that material enjoyment is pregnant with misery; the delivery is only a matter of "when, not if?". The devotees of the Lord are often more merciful than the Lord; one way their extra mercy manifests is in their forceful enunciation of the Lord's teachings. "There is no point in arguing that a materialistic man can be happy." This is one of those quotes of Srila Prabhupada that, by its sheer conviction, jolts us out of our complacency in material life. Most of the media and culture around us is vigorously propagating that materialism is *the* way to become happy, but Srila Prabhupada asserts with absolute conviction that materialism can never make anyone happy.

Srila Prabhupada is simply rephrasing an essential and repeated teaching of the Lord. To help us grasp this scriptural teaching, Srila Prabhupada would often tell the parable of a fish.

A fish lived naturally and happily in the ocean. But somehow it got allured out of the water, being captivated by the mirages that it saw on the land. It started feeling restless from the moment it came out of the water and continued suffering till the moment it returned back. And the further it went away from the ocean in the pursuit of pleasure, the more became its suffering and the greater the effort needed to end that suffering.

give the analogy of a fish: just as a fish starts suffering the moment it leaves the ocean, we start suffering the moment we leave the nectar-ocean of Krishna consciousness. Let us reflect on this analogy a bit.

The Fate of the Fish

Imagine a fish in an ocean bordering a vast desert. It sees a mirage onshore and decides one day that life on land will be more enjoyable. From the moment it comes out of the ocean, its suffering begins. The mirage provides no water, and any drops of water it finds are too small to give any satisfaction. The only way the fish can experience happiness is by returning to the ocean. The more it pursues either the mirage or the drops of water, the more it suffers from the scorching heat of the sand underneath and the sun overhead. Had the fish known it would be miserable the moment it left the ocean, it would not have ventured onshore and would have ignored the mirage. Even if it didn't feel completely happy in the water, the way to greater happiness was never to be found on land.

All of us are like the fish and Krishna consciousness is like the ocean. From the moment we let our consciousness come out of the nectar-ocean of Krishna consciousness, we begin experiencing misery. We are allured out of Krishna consciousness by the sense objects: pleasures and treasures, positions and possessions. No matter how good-looking the sense objects seem to be, they are simply a sham and can never make us happy. They are temporarily pleasure-giving, whereas we are eternally pleasure-seeking. The only way we can experience happiness is by returning to Krishna consciousness. The more we pursue the sense objects, the longer we suffer as we journey to and fro between Krishna consciousness and the sense objects through the scorching heat of the materialistic conditioning internally and the material conditions externally. This journey is painful and difficult because every action that we perform conditions us, implicates us into patterns of thinking and behaving that incite us to repeat that action. The human vulnerability to conditioning traps us in addiction—often unwittingly and sometimes even unwillingly.

That's why, by the time we do realize that material enjoyment is futile, it has often become the default setting of our mind; we instinctively, unthinkingly gravitate toward it, and going against that gravitational force becomes difficult and often painful. Moreover, in the pursuit of material enjoyment, we mix and bond with materialistically oriented people, and the emotional bonds we thus form often make it tough for us to turn away from worldly pleasures that have won us others' approval.

Therefore, when we know we are going to increase our misery by coming out of Krishna consciousness, why then should we ever come out? Indeed, why should we even cast a glance at the sense objects that might beguile us to come out? Even if we don't feel sufficiently happy in Krishna consciousness, the only way to greater happiness is not outwards, but inwards; not out of Krishna consciousness, but deeper into Krishna consciousness.

Noteworthy Nuances

Of course, the fish analogy is not perfect. In fact, no material analogy can ever perfectly convey a spiritual truth. But as long as we are at our present material level of consciousness, we can think of only material objects and concepts. So, if the spiritual teachers did not use material analogies, then we would find it extremely hard to grasp spiritual truths. Therefore, they use material analogies to convey spiritual truths – even if imperfectly. To avoid any misconceptions due to the incidental imperfections of the fish analogy, let us consider its limitations. In fact, these qualifications reveal important nuances of the philosophy of Krishna consciousness:

1. When the fish comes out of the water, within a short time, it dies. We being eternal souls never die, but by forsaking Krishna consciousness we "kill" our spiritual awareness: the awareness that we are spiritual beings entitled to

spiritual happiness in the spiritual world by reciprocating spiritual love with the supreme spiritual reality, Krishna. Those who kill their spiritual awareness are referred to in the Srimad Bhagavatam and the Ishopanishad by the apt metaphorical term "atma-ha", killers of the soul.

2. A fish is never allured by a mirage, but we are attracted by the mirage-like sense objects. This is due to the power of Maya, the illusion-causing energy that perverts our perception by its twofold potencies:

    a. Avaranatmika-shakti (covering potency): This potency obscures our perception of our true nature as spiritual beings and freezes our spiritual desires

    b. Prakshematika-shakti (kicking potency): This potency deludes us with the false self-conception that we are materialistic creatures and kindles our material desires.

3. The suffering of a fish out of water is always easy to see, but the suffering of people devoid of Krishna consciousness may not be so easy to see. Factually, no one can be happy without Krishna consciousness and the statistics quoted at the start are a poignant demonstration of this eternal truth. But those living beings who have been living without Krishna consciousness for a long, long time have almost entirely forgotten the taste of Krishna consciousness. As they presently don't know any pleasure other than the pseudo-pleasure of sense gratification, they have become habituated to this pseudo-pleasure despite all the miseries that precede and succeed it. Habituated thus, they don't

know their own misery and so don't seem miserable. This is confirmed in the Srimad Bhagavatam (3.30.5), "The conditioned living entity is satisfied in his own particular species of life; while deluded by the covering influence of the illusory energy, he feels little inclined to cast off his body, even when in hell, for he takes delight in hellish enjoyment."

Due to this power of illusion, materialistic people may seem temporarily happy, though they aren't. And this apparition may beguile even spiritually-minded people into materialistic pursuits and to alternate between material enjoyment and spiritual purification. But those of us who know something better, who have recently tasted Krishna consciousness, can no longer be satisfied with the illusory tastes of sense gratification. Why? Because the sublime and supreme taste of Krishna consciousness is still fresh in our memory – if not in our conscious memory, then at least in our subconscious memory. That's why even if we consciously turn away from Krishna consciousness to pursue sense gratification, we subconsciously keep comparing the taste of sense gratification with the taste of Krishna consciousness and naturally find the former unsatisfying. That's why the Bhagavatam (1.5.19) proclaims, "Even though a devotee of Lord Krishna sometimes falls down somehow or other, he certainly does not undergo material existence like others because a person who has once relished the taste of the lotus feet of the Lord can do nothing but remember that ecstasy again and again."

Unfortunately, despite repeatedly experiencing sense

gratification to be insipid and inane, our stubborn mind may still impel and compel us to keep pursuing it. In such situations, we can use the graphic fish analogy and the resonant Prabhupada quote as the hammers for driving in the nail-like truth of the futility of sense gratification through the wall-like stubbornness of our mind. Sooner or later we will realize that the pursuit of sense gratification is a lost cause and will turn – rather re-turn – to Krishna consciousness. And better sooner than later.

Science

The God Particle: Is There Anything godly About It?

"Does 'the God particle' disprove the existence of God?" a young man asked me after a recent talk.

"The so-called God particle," I answered, "has zero charge, zero spin, and a near-zero lifespan; it exists for less than a trillionth of a second. Does that sound like God to you?"

"No, not really," replied the questioner, taken aback.

"Exactly," I said emphatically. "Its discovery has very little bearing on the existence of God; it is just one step forward in the Standard Model, which is just one theory that deals with quantum physics, which is just one branch   of physics, which is just one branch of science, which is just one area of human knowledge that deals with material nature, which is just one slice of reality."

I had anticipated questions on this topic and so was prepared.

"Let me quote theoretical physicist Michio Kaku, who writes in the *Wall Street Journal,* in an article entitled *The 'God Particle' and the Origins of the Universe*:

[extract]

The Standard Model only gives us a crude approximation of the rich diversity found in the universe. One embarrassing omission is that the Standard Model makes no mention of gravity, even though gravity holds the Earth and the sun together. In fact, the Standard Model only describes 4% of the matter and energy of the universe (the rest being mysterious dark matter and dark energy).

From a strictly aesthetic point of view, the Standard Model is also rather ugly. The various subatomic particles look like they have been slapped together haphazardly. It is a theory that only a mother could love, and even its creators have admitted that it is only a piece of the true, final theory.

[end extract]

"So the theory is neither complete nor elegant," I added. "And if even the full theory doesn't have any of the attributes of God, what then to speak of one particle within the theory?"

Looking a bit unsure, he asked, "Then why is the particle called 'the God particle'?"

"Good question. Actually, there is nothing godly about the particle. The name is a deliberately chosen misnomer. The particle is technically known as Higgs boson, named after the two scientists— England's Peter Higgs and India's Satyendranath Bose—who were instrumental in postulating it. When physicist Leon Lederman wrote a book about the particle, his publisher told him the subject was too esoteric to have much appeal. So, like expert spin doctors, they came up with a name that would catch the public imagination: 'the God particle.' Most scientists dislike the name, knowing that it overemphasizes the particle's importance. Science writer John Horgan highlights the inappropriateness of the name on a *Scientific American* blog: 'This is scientific hype at its most outrageous. If the Higgs is the "God Particle," what should we call an even more fundamental particle, like a string? The Godhead Particle? The Mother of God Particle?'

"Although the name is inapt, it has stuck in the media. And the name is one important reason why the discovery has attracted so much attention. Not to discredit the hard work of the scientists who have done the research, but do we have to be misled by the hype?"

"No," replied my questioner, satisfied.

The Godly Particle

Later, as I pondered the issue, it struck me that something godly could indeed be derived from "the God particle"; it could be used to draw attention to the actual godly particle, the soul, which the *Bhagavad-gita* (15.7) says is an eternal fragmental part of God. Research into the infinitesimal quantum particle has rich parallels with research into the infinitesimal spiritual particle, the soul. In fact, I noticed that the whole field of modern science has broad similarities with the field of Vedic spirituality.

Here are four of those similarities:

1. Things are not as they appear;

2. The unapparent is stunningly greater than the apparent;

3. The unapparent can be known not by ordinary ways, but only by ways appropriate to it;

4. The appropriate ways require instruments and qualifications.

1. Things are not as they appear:

Scientists today dismiss derisively as naïve realism the idea that the world is as it appears. The scientific eye sees things far differently from the normal eye. For example, consider the desk in front of me.

It seems solid, but science says it's mostly empty space. It seems static, but science says it's filled with electrons whirling around their nuclei a million billion times a second.

Like modern scientists, Vedic spiritualists also assert that all is not as it seems. For example, let's consider the physical body. It seems to be the source of life, but Vedic savants say it isn't. The *Bhagavad-gītā* (2.17) states that life originates in the soul, which sends a current of consciousness streaming through the body and thereby animates the body's biochemical machinery.

2. The unapparent is stunningly greater than the apparent:

Science holds that the layers of existence inaccessible to our senses are far greater than those that are accessible. For example, the visible frequencies comprise only a tiny, narrow band within the greater spectrum of electromagnetic waves. For that matter, half an ounce of water spilled on a table seems insignificant to our eyes, but beyond what our eyes can see, that drop contains 6.023×10^{23}—roughly 600,000 billion billion—molecules.

Like modern science, Vedic spirituality states that what eludes the eye is far greater than what meets it. The spiritual level of existence is much greater and grander than the material. And the happiness available at that spiritual level likewise exceeds the material by millions of times. In fact, the *Srimad-Bhagavatam* proclaims that spiritual happiness is so oceanically great that in contrast the most intense material enjoyment seems as insignificant as a puddle.

3.   The unapparent can be known not by ordinary ways, but only by ways appropriate to it:

The adage "Seeing is believing" has historically been popular as a polemical tool among religion-bashers: "Show me God and the soul, and then I will believe you." But today's scientists find themselves at the receiving end of this same old anti-religious jab: "Show me the Higgs boson, and then I will believe you." And scientists have to respond by using the same argument religionists have always used: "It cannot be seen with the eyes, but can be perceived only by ways suitable to it."

4.   The appropriate ways require instruments and qualifications:

In modern science, perceiving the Higgs boson requires ultra-sophisticated instruments. In fact, it requires the world's most expensive and elaborate instrument: the $10.5 billion Large Hadron Collider, housed in an eighteen-mile tunnel buried deep underground near the French-Swiss border. In addition to the instrument, ten thousand scientists engaged in years of study, training, and laboratory experience are also required to comprehend the workings and the readings of the instrument. To anyone without these qualifications, the patterns on the sensors that detected the Higgs boson will make little, if any, sense.

Similarly, in Vedic spirituality, perceiving the soul requires a sophisticated instrument, albeit an internal one: a finely tuned consciousness situated in an evolved state called *samadhi*. Also, to discern the evidences as they appear on the sensor of the consciousness requires a systematic study of spiritual philosophy and a diligent practice of meditation techniques. To anyone without these qualifications, the changes in consciousness will make little, if any, sense.

More Incentives

Given these substantial parallels, there's a strong case to be made that intelligent, enterprising people are needed to embark on research into the godly particle. In fact, there are additional incentives for soul research that are absent in particle physics research:

1. No expense:

The Higgs boson research is stupendously expensive (or scandalously so, depending on one's perspective), requiring as it does billions of dollars. John Horgan, in the above-mentioned article, states that the U.S. government closed down a similar instrument in America (the Superconducting Supercollider) because it "was sucking up tax dollars faster than a black hole." But in comforting contrast, soul research doesn't require any significant expense. One's consciousness just needs to be refined using time-honored meditation techniques centered on the Hare Krishna mantra, available for free.

2. Individual verification:

Most of us are not specialists in particle physics, and so we do not have the expensive and complex scientific education necessary to personally verify the existence of the Higgs boson. We have to accept its existence as an article of faith. But all of us can individually practice the simple meditation practices and experientially verify the existence of the soul. This is the bold invitational approach of the *Bhagavad-gîtå* (9.2): Though the existence of the soul may seem initially like an article of faith, it soon becomes a living reality. In fact, over time we realize that the soul is the foremost of all realities, the ground reality that enables us to perceive and experience the world we are accustomed to honoring with the word "real."

3. Meaning-enriching:

Most scientists are unclear about how the discovery of the Higgs boson is going to practically benefit humanity. They suggest that it may possibly lead to the development of better technologies. Even if it does, it still won't add anything to our understanding of the meaning, value, or purpose of life. In fact, the whole arena of particle physics is radically disconnected from the world we live in. David Berlinski, in his book *The Devil's Delusion,* points this out poignantly:

"Over *there,* fields are pregnant with latent energy, particles flicker into existence and disappear . . . time and space contract into some sort of agitated quantum foam. Nothing is continuous. Nothing stays the same for long, except the electrons, and they are identical, like porcelain Chinese soldiers. A pointless frenzy prevails throughout. Over *here,* space and time are stable and continuous. Matter is what it is, and energy is what it does. There are solid and enduring shapes and forms. . . . Changes appear slowly, but even when rapid, they appear in stable patterns. There is dazzling variety throughout."

He concludes the contrast by underscoring that scientists have "no idea whatsoever how the ordered physical, moral, mental, aesthetic, and social world . . . could have ever arisen from the seething anarchy of the elementary particles. It is like imagining sea foam resolving itself into the Parthenon."

The discovery of the soul, however, can bring immense meaning and immediate purpose into our lives. Nobel Laureate brain scientist Roger Sperry pointed out, "Beliefs concerning the ultimate purposes and meaning of life and the accompanying world view perspectives that mold beliefs of right and wrong are critically dependent . . . on concepts regarding the conscious self."

The discovery of the soul will help us understand that we are not fragile bags of matter doomed to destruction after some feverish flapping in the tiny span of allotted time that is our present life. We will understand that we are indestructible souls destined for eternal happiness. All of us can reclaim that glorious destiny by wisely using our present lifetime for doing soul research and thereby transforming our lifespan into a launching pad for takeoff into immortality. This realization of our spiritual identity can also help us in this world: It can restore a sustainable balance between material and spiritual values in our lives, and thereby free us from the excessive materialism jeopardizing our economy and ecology today.

Can any discovery be as significant as that?

Artificial Life? Why Not Real Life?

(Co-authored with Caitanya Carana Das and Ayush Goyal, University of Oxford Biologist)

"Scientists create artificial life," declared newspaper headlines around the world in May 2010. Genome pioneer J. Craig Venter, the man behind the sensation, claimed, "This is a philosophical advance as much as a technical advance."

What exactly did Venter do? He:

1. Determined the sequence of the DNA in one of the world's simplest bacteria,

2. Synthesized a copy of that DNA from components sold by a biological supply company,

3. Replaced the natural DNA in a living bacterial cell with this synthetic DNA.

DNA (deoxyribonucleic acid) is a long linear molecule found in the nucleus of a cell. Sometimes dubbed as the king of molecules, DNA comprises of genes or biological units of heredity that are passed down from parent to offspring. The complete DNA (also known as the genome) has a few billion chemical bases (bases are specific bio-molecules) paired together into a double helix. The four bases used in DNA (adenine, guanine, thymine and cytosine) act like the letters of an alphabet, and the specific sequences of these bases convey information used for building proteins (chemical compounds used by living cells). The actual production of proteins is done by "gene expression" machinery within the cell that makes copies of the genes and uses the information therein to arrange amino acids (the building blocks of proteins) into the sequence and structure required for the protein under production. Each different gene sequence results in a protein with a distinct structure and shape, and consequently distinct function in the cell.

Venter, like many modern scientists, believes in reductionism: the idea that all the features of a complex system can be explained in terms of or "reduced" down to the properties of its simple components. Reductionist biologists hold that a living organism is like a computer: just as the capacities of the computer can be explained in terms of the capacities of its components, the characteristics, traits, behaviors of livings organisms can be explained in terms of their components, going down ultimately to their genes. As Oxford biologist Richard Dawkins noted, "The machine code of the genes is uncannily computer-like." Applying the computer analogy to the current experiment, Venter has certainly not created the complete computer. What he has done – introducing a new genetic sequence within a preexisting living organism – is like replacing one chip within a pre-existing computer by another chip. So, even from this reductionist viewpoint, he has not created life. That's why Caltech biologist and Nobel laureate, David Baltimore, pointed out that Venter has "overplayed the importance" of his results; he "has not created life, only mimicked it."

What if scientists someday use the biochemical components to create the entire cell? Would that amount to creating life? No, because that would just be like making the computer, not the person who would use the computer. Although reductionist scientists would have us believe that there is no such "person" and that life is just a product of bio-chemicals, living systems behave in ways fundamentally and inexplicably different from nonliving objects. Nonliving objects are created, deteriorate over time and eventually meet with destruction. Living systems exhibits three additional features: maintenance, growth and reproduction. A living human hand, if cut, can clot and heal itself; the most state-of-the-art artificial hand, if cut, cannot clot or heal itself. The simplest unicellular organism can grow; the most sophisticated computer cannot. The most primitive living systems can reproduce; even the most advanced robots can't.

No wonder Boston University bioengineer James Collins candidly admitted the scientific ground reality: "Scientists don't know enough about biology to create life."

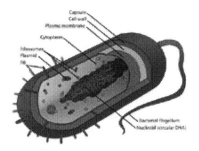

The Program of Life

What is amiss in the reductionist portrayal of life is analyzed by eminent Oxford biologist Denis Noble, renowned for his contributions to physiology, in his book *The Music of Life*. He points out an important problem with the notion of DNA as the "program or blueprint of life". This notion that deifies DNA into the super-agent behind life is implicit in the current claims about creation of artificial life. Noble explains that the DNA is more like a database than a program; in computer terminology, a database refers to an organized storage of data, whereas a program refers to a list of executable instructions that achieve a specific objective. The DNA only contains data, but this data is useless unless it is read by "gene expression" cellular machinery that actually executes the "program of life" to build proteins. The database-like role of DNA is evident from the fact that the same gene sequence code of the DNA can be converted to different proteins according to the needs of the particular cell that it is in. Therefore, the genes do not determine all the functions of the cell, but are simply templates that are interpreted into differently functioning and distinct proteins depending on the environment and need of the cell. To complete the computer analogy then, the cell is a computer, the cell nucleus is the controller (control unit that manages the entire operation of the cell), DNA is the database that contains genetic memory data and program data, protein production is the program (the biological tasks to be completed to build proteins), gene expression mechanism is the processing unit, and proteins are the output.

The Music of Life

Noble illustrates the limitation of the reductionist view by another intriguing analogy. Let us say, a person relaxes at home by playing a music CD. Upon hearing the music, tears flow from the person's eyes. Imagine aliens observing this scene. The alien scientists enquiring about the cause of the tears trace it back to the speaker system, to the CD player, to the CD, to the particular track being played. By their empirical scientific method, they reason that the music and the subsequent tears were caused by the digital information encoded in the CD track being played. All of us know that the emotions are caused not by the CD track itself, but by the context and memories attached to the melody, the song, the players and other such factors. The music does not originate from the CD but from the musician who recorded it onto the CD. The music is independent of the CD, which is only one of the various forms of media that allow the music to be stored and played. Echoing Noble's reasoning, French philosopher Andre Pichot asserts that the DNA-mania of modern geneticists is similar to the aliens' hasty reasoning. As the CD is useless without the CD player, the DNA is useless without the gene expression cellular machinery that copies and converts the gene code into proteins. Just as the CD is only a media for storing music, DNA is only a media for storing and recreating biological life. DNA is neither life nor the absolute cause of life, just as the CD music track is neither the music nor the primal cause of the music. Life is thus like music: neither can be reduced down to codes – biological or digital. DNA is like the CD track; DNA stores biological data for creating proteins, the CD track stores digital data for creating sounds. Like music, life does not originate from and is independent of the media temporarily used for data storage.

Then, where does life originate from? Just as music can only originate from a musician, life can only originate from a living person. That living person, according to the Vedas, is the spirit soul. The Bhagavad-gita (2.17) explains that the soul is an irreducible, eternal unit of consciousness. When the soul enters a biological medium such as our body, the body acquires apparent life. Just as a living person is necessary to play the CD and the CD player, the soul is necessary for the dead inert cellular machinery to read the DNA genetic code and run the biochemical processes that animate the cell. The soul is the cause of maintenance, growth and reproduction, the features of living systems that defy reductionist explanation as discussed earlier. The Gita (2.25) explains that the soul is "invisible and inconceivable", implying that its presence cannot be detected by our senses and sense-created instruments.

The Gita (13.33-34) also points out that the soul remains distinct from the body it animates, as does sunlight illuminating the universe or air pervading space. So, when a part of the body is changed, the soul remains unchanged, just as when a component in a computer is changed, the computer-user remaining unchanged. Thus, in Venter's experiment, the soul animating the bacteria remained unchanged when the DNA within that bacteria was changed.

Reductionist philosophers object to the existence of any non-material spirit animating the body because, they hold, spirit that being of a nature fundamentally different from matter cannot influence matter. The Gita agrees that spirit can't influence matter, but asserts that the Supreme Spirit being the controller of both matter and spirit can. The Gita (13.23) explains that spirit interacts with matter through the agency of the Supersoul, an expansion of God who is immanent and all-pervading in matter.

In this connection, it is pertinent to note that Cambridge-educated researcher Stephen Meyer in his book *Signature in the Cell* explains how attempts of reductionist scientists to explain life in biological terms has paradoxically ended up showing the need for intelligence as the cause of life. For example, computer algorithms that attempted to simulate genetic information by random symbol generation achieved modest success only when they were intelligently directed toward a pre-chosen target sequence. Thus, far from proving the efficacy of randomness, they ended up proving the necessity of intelligence in generating genetic information. Could the same apply in Venter's case? Intelligent scientists working for decades with funding running into millions were able to synthesize only one of the simplest DNAs. What does that say about the intelligence required to synthesize DNAs as complex as the human genome? Author George Sim Johnson points out, "Human DNA contains more organized information than the encyclopedia Britannica. If the full text of the encyclopedia were to arrive in computer code from outer space, most people would regard it as proof of the existence of extraterrestrial intelligence." Obviously then, the organized information in the DNA can be regarded as proof of a magnificent designing intelligence, as Meyer persuasively established in his book. This echoes the Gita (9.10), which states that material nature works under God's supervision.

Playing God

Despite his claims to be "playing God", Venter has unwittingly played into the hands of God by providing evidence for his existence and intelligence. Historically, attempts to play God have repeatedly backfired. In new fields of research, scientists almost invariably promise beneficial, often sensational, future results. However, the past track record of such promises shows counterproductive, often devastating, consequences. In the field of genetic engineering itself, genetically-modified (GM) food was advertised as the solution to world hunger, but it ended up causing hunger-deaths of hundreds of farmers in Maharashtra, India. These farmers were captivated by promises of pest-resistant seeds and high yields, but when the pests developed resistance to the seeds, the yields failed utterly. Moreover, as the GM seeds are designed to not give seeds for the next sowing, the farmers had no chance of a yield in the next season either. Afflicted by poverty, hunger and hopelessness, multitudes of them committed suicide. Concerned with the health hazards associated with GM food, the European Union has banned its use. NGOs are attempting to have similar curbs on GM food in other parts of the world.

What are the possible dangers in "artificial life" research?

Genome manipulation of the kind done by Venter can lead to the development of medicine-resistant variants of disease-producing microbes, which could trigger a pandemic. The genome Venter synthesized was copied from a natural bacterium that infects goats. Before copying the DNA, he claims to have excised fourteen genes likely to be pathogenic, so that the new bacterium, even if it escaped, would be unlikely to cause goats harm. However, such measures may not be incorporated in future similar researches – either unintentionally or intentionally. Will we then see headlines of "artificial deaths" – deaths caused by human attempts at creating artificial life – in the papers? While some may consider such a scenario unlikely and even unduly pessimistic, it is certainly a possibility. And perhaps contemplation on the worst-case possibility is necessary to prevent it from becoming a reality.

Real Life

On a positive note, the "artificial life" news, by bringing to the forefront the age-old question of what life actually is, may prompt some soul-searching – at least figuratively and maybe even literally. Developing the computer analogy further, ISKCON scientist the late Dr Richard L Thompson (Sadaputa Dasa), in his book "Maya: The World as a Virtual Reality", explains how our entire present existence is like a computer simulation, a virtual reality. So as spiritual beings, the material existence that we are currently leading is itself an artificial life. From that perspective, the attempt to create artificial life within an artificial life is little more than an artifice. Alternative to such artifices is the spiritual technology described in the Gita that can enable us to progress from our current artificial life to our real life as eternal beings. If the energy spent on creating artificial life were directed to cultivate spiritual knowledge and practice, humanity would make quantum leaps in its understanding of life. The scientific establishment may or may not do this, but each of us individually can. Then we will no longer be taken in by overhyped reports about artificial life, for we will be constantly experiencing and relishing the meaning of real life – and will want to share that with everyone.

Are we mistaking scientism to be science?

Question: When I talk about God, soul, rebirth, people often question why discuss such unscientific things in this modern age of science?

Answer: Their question betrays their basic misconception: science has a monopoly on human knowledge, and only things that are "scientific" are true. This misconception is not a result of science, but of scientism, the peculiar school of thought that places around science a halo of "omniscience." However, scientism itself is unscientific! There is no scientific experiment to prove that scientific knowledge is the only true knowledge. Thus, their question itself, being based on an unscientific assumption, is not scientific. So, if they feel that people should not discuss unscientific things, then firstly they themselves should stop raising this question.

Nonetheless, now that the question has been raised, let's explore its answer further. Pointing out the proper place of science in humanity's quest for knowledge is sometimes misunderstood as an insult to science and to the human intellect itself. But far from being an insult, it is a tribute to the human intellect. The same extraordinary human intellect that has led us humans to the heights of scientific knowledge has also led us to remarkable insights in many other fields. As Albert Einstein stated, "All religions, arts and sciences are branches of the same tree." By acknowledging this all-round accomplishment of the human intellect and not letting scientism monopolize human knowledge, we open for ourselves the door to a holistic understanding of ourselves and the world we live in.

Question: But isn't science the most reliable way of acquiring knowledge?

Answer: That depends on the field one is considering. Noble Laureate Physicist Erwin Schrodinger eloquently stated the abilities and the inabilities of science: "I am very astonished that the scientific picture of the real world around me is very deficient. It gives a lot of factual information, puts all our experience in a magnificently consistent order, but it is ghastly silent about all and sundry that is really near to our heart, that really matters to us. It cannot tell us a word about red and blue, bitter and sweet, physical pain and physical delight; it knows nothing of beautiful and ugly, good or bad, God and eternity. Science sometimes pretends to answer questions in these domains, but the answers are very often so silly that we are not inclined to take them seriously." To better appreciate Schrodinger's remark, let's consider an example. Suppose a brain surgeon returns home to find his wife upset with him. If science were to be his only means of acquiring knowledge, he would have to do a brain scan of his wife to find why she is annoyed. Would that help? Obviously not; it would compound his wife's annoyance into anger.

Here's another example. Consider the experience of seeing a beautiful sunset. We can directly experience the beauty of the sunset. But can any scientific experiment measure that beauty? Science could perhaps measure some parameters like the intensity of the sunlight, but such measurements would do little to convey or explain the actual experience of the beauty.

To summarize, science does have its utility and authority in certain fields, but extrapolating that authority to judge all fields of knowledge is unwarranted, unproductive, and sometime even counterproductive. We can save ourselves from the misleading spell of scientism while simultaneously maintaining due respect for science by bringing to mind the sage advice of Copernicus about what constitutes knowledge: "To know that we know what we know, and to know that we do not know what we do not know, that is true knowledge."

Question: Isn't science more reliable than other branches of knowledge because it deals with factual things?

Answer: Science doesn't reserve itself to the study of factual things, if by factual, we mean things that are seen by our eyes or otherwise perceived by our senses. Let's see just two categories of such areas of study within science

1. **Study of unperceivable objects**: Most of the objects studied in modern physics are not perceivable at all: electrons, mesons, neutrinos, hadrons, to name a few. Moreover, in some cases, this non-perceivability is not just a practical limitation imposed by insufficiently sophisticated instruments. Quarks, for example, are considered non-perceivable even in principle; they are so tightly bound inside the protons and neutrons that nothing can make them break out on their own. Yet all these particles are treated as scientifically factual, and their existence and behavior is given as a scientific explanation for many direct physical observations.

2. **Study of abstract mathematical conceptions**: Additionally, with the increasing use of mathematics in physics, the gap between the concepts studied by science and the factual objects of the world has widened. This trend

was noted by Nikola Tesla nearly a century ago: "Today's scientists have substituted mathematics for experiments, and they wander off through equation after equation, and eventually build a structure which has no relation to reality." Since Tesla'-s made this insightful observation, the trend has only aggravated further.

Question: Isn't scientific knowledge more reliable because it is objective? After all, the observations of one scientist can be verified by others.

Answer: The reliability of scientific knowledge is problematized by several factors such as the following

1. **Difficult to verify**: Not all scientific observations are so easily verifiable. For example, when physicists claim to have observed a fundamental particle using a high-energy particle accelerator, their observation can be verified only by those who have access to those expensive equipments and can understand the complex technical jargon intrinsic in the claim of the observation.

2. **Impossible to observe**: Further, in quantum physics, objectivity is widely thought of as impossible because the very act of observation is said to change the observed object.

3. **Subjective bias in observation**: Moreover, observations are not as objective as they seem to be, as is pointed out by the English astronomer Arthur Eddington: "A scientist commonly professes to base his beliefs on observations, not theories. Theories, it is said, are useful

in suggesting new ideas and new lines of investigation for the experimenter; but 'hard facts' are the only proper ground for conclusion. I have never come across anyone who carries this profession into practice – certainly not the hard-headed experimentalist, who is the more swayed by his theories because he is less accustomed to scrutinize them... It is better to admit frankly that theory has, and is entitled to have, an important share in determining belief." The pioneering quantum physicist Max Planck was even more forthright in stating the role of subjectivity: "A new scientific truth does not triumph by convincing its opponents and making them see light, but rather because its opponents die, and a new generation grows up that is familiar with it." The subjectivity inherent within the scientific enterprise is systematically documented by historian of science Thomas Kuhn in his eye-opening book The Structure of Scientific Revolutions. He shows that scientists, like the rest of us, are also fallible human beings, who are often motivated by their personal interests and preconceptions, constricted by the beliefs and biases of their superiors, subject to peer pressure and concerned about the availability and continuance of research grants.

Question: Isn't scientific knowledge preferable because it is free from dependence on faith?

Answer: Science demands faith both in its general method as well as in its specific theories. Let's analyze a few of the elements of faith in science:

1. **Its underlying assumptions:** Consider the following statement of physicist Gerald't Hooft: "We [physicists]

are trying to uncover more of that [the universality of our scientific theories]. It is our belief that there is more." Obviously, "our belief" means "our faith." Scientific research is based on the implicit faith that nature behaves according to laws that can be uncovered by human intelligence. This implicit faith is just an assumption without any actual proof or without even any theoretical possibility of proof. In fact, the behavior of many of the fundamental particles in atomic physics defies description by any scientific laws. Nonetheless, physicists toil on hoping to find out some such laws in the future. To hope for the existence of unseen and unproven things: isn't that what faith is all about?

2.   **Its dependence on the inductive method**: Moreover, most scientific knowledge is acquired using the inductive method, in which patterns discerned from finite observations are extrapolated into universal laws. The 18th century Scottish philosopher David Hume argued powerfully that the use of induction can never be rationally justified, and his arguments have never been persuasively refuted. Inductive reasoning is thus a fundamental, indispensable article of faith in science.

3.   **Its use of hypothesis**: Further, when scientists propose a specific hypothesis to explain a set of observations, they have faith that their hypothesis is correct and that it will be verified by future observations. Often, even when subsequent observations don't support the hypothesis, they continue to believe it, hoping that future observations will. For example, evolutionists believe that all species have evolved from a common ancestor, but the fossil record doesn't show any evidence of transitional links

(intermediate species that are supposed to have existed in the past and that formed the evolutionary link between two existing species). So, some evolutionists claim that evolution occurs too slowly to be seen by the human eye, and too fast to be seen in the fossil record. Even the most dull-witted person can understand what this claim boils down to: faith – faith despite the absence of supporting evidence.

4. **Its hype among the masses**: Far greater than the faith that scientists require in their research is the faith that common people have in the findings of scientists. The extent of unquestioning faith that scientific findings command is seen in the following observation of Einstein: "Tell a man that there are 300 billion stars in the universe, and he'll believe you.... Tell him that a bench has wet paint upon it and he'll have to touch it to be sure."

Question: Isn't science special because it follows the scientific method?

Answer: Let's consider the typical steps that comprise the scientific method:

1. Observe some aspect of the universe.

2. Form a hypothesis that potentially explains the observation.

3. Devise testable predictions from that hypothesis.

4. Conduct experiments that can test those predictions.

5. Modify the hypothesis until it is in accord with all

observations and predictions.

6.   Arrive at a conclusion of whether the hypothesis is true or not.

Now consider the reasoning of a cricket fan:

1.   Observation: A cricketer X hits sixers frequently.

2.   Hypothesis: His ability to hit frequent sixers is due to his strong arms and his swift, smooth arm swing.

3.   Experiment: When cricketers with strong arms and swift, smooth arm swing are examined, they are seen to hit sixers frequently. When cricketers without these bodily attributes are examined, they are seen to not hit sixers so frequently.

4.   Conclusion: Hypothesis confirmed.

Clearly, the above reasoning parallels, in an abbreviated way, the scientific method. This parallel shows that the much-touted scientific method is not unique to science; it can be used and is often used in many other fields. In fact, the scientific method is nothing more than a systematized version of common sense, as is confirmed by Albert Einstein, "The whole of science is nothing more than a refinement of everyday thinking." Just as common sense can give us right answers, so can science. And just as common sense can give us wrong answers, so can science. That's why the notion that scientific knowledge special and privileged because it is acquired using some reverence-worthy "scientific method" is fallacious. There's no such method.

Question: Isn't the fact that science works the proof of the truth of scientific knowledge?

Answer: The history of science reveals many theories that worked, but were subsequently shown to be wrong. The phlogiston theory of combustion is a classic example. Oxford University Press' *Philosophy of Science* explains: "This theory, which was widely accepted until the end of the 18th century, held that when any substance burns, it releases a substance called 'phlogiston' into the atmosphere. Modern chemistry teaches that this is false: there is no such substance as phlogiston. Rather, burning occurs when things react with oxygen in the air. But despite the non-existence of phlogiston, the phlogiston theory was empirically quite successful: it fitted the observational data available at the time quite well." The American philosopher of science Larry Laudan has listed more than 30 such theories that worked, but were wrong. Many modern scientific theories have met the same fate, but because these are generally phrased in technical jargon and mathematical symbols, most people are unable to even understand what the theories are, leave alone understand how they have been shown to be wrong.

Question: Do you mean to say that all scientific knowledge is wrong?

Answer: Not at all. Scientific knowledge has its utility and value. Scientific technology has astonishingly transformed almost every aspect of our daily living. Science should undoubtedly be given credit where credit is due. At the same time, understanding how science works helps us to see its findings in proper perspective. In the vast panorama of sensations that nature presents us, scientists choose in advance their parameters of study: the measurable, quantifiable properties of nature. While this approach helps in manipulating a certain slice of nature, it gives a significantly incomplete picture of reality. That's why philosopher of science Karl Popper remarked, "Science may be described as the art of systematic oversimplification."

The reputed physicist Fritjof Capra in his well-known book *The Tao of Physics* explains how science is like a map. Just as a map helps – and helps immensely – in navigating the mapped territory, science helps in manipulating the physical world. However, a map, no matter how exhaustive, is neither the territory, nor a complete description of the territory. Similarly, science, no matter how exhaustive, is neither the reality, nor a complete description of the reality. If the map helps us to precisely reach a particular house in a city, where we meet the owner of the house, will we decide that the owner of the house is non-existent and imaginary because he is not shown in our map? Obviously not. We will recognize that the map has now served its purpose and will switch to another knowledge-source, perhaps skillful communication, to know more about the owner. Similarly, science may efficiently guide us in our exploration of the physical world, but when we encounter essential features of our world that are not found in the world of science –emotions, consciousness, free will, the quest for meaning and purpose, should we reject these features as unscientific and therefore unreal? Obviously not. We should instead seek other knowledge-sources that help us know more about these features.

The danger of scientism, of mistaking the map to be the territory, is eloquently stated by former US President Theodore Roosevelt: "There is superstition in science quite as much as there is superstition in theology, and it is all the more dangerous because those suffering from it are profoundly convinced that they are freeing themselves from all superstition. No grotesque repulsiveness of medieval superstition, even as it survived into nineteenth-century Spain and Naples, could be much more intolerant, much more destructive of all that is fine in morality, in the spiritual sense, and indeed in civilization itself, than that hard dogmatic materialism of today which often not merely calls itself scientific but arrogates to itself the sole right to use the term. If these pretensions affected only scientific men themselves, it would be a matter of small moment, but unfortunately they tend gradually to affect the whole people, and to establish a very dangerous standard of private and public conduct in the public mind."

Question: Can science by its onward march discover spiritual principles?

Answer: Every field of knowledge has its own distinctive methods. Attempting to gain knowledge of that field without adopting its methods is generally difficult and sometimes impossible, especially with regards to advanced concepts in that field. To illustrate, let's consider different scientific instruments of increasing complexity:

1. We can measure our bodily weight quickly using a weighing machine. However, to measure the weight without using the machine or similar device, we have to adopt the cumbersome process of standing on one side of a weighing scale and stacking one kg weights on the other side until the two sides balance.

2. We can measure the distance from the earth of a particular star in a distant galaxy with a telescope. However, to measure that distance without using the telescope or some similar device, we have to adopt the expensive and impractical process of boarding a spacecraft and flying

until there while keeping an eye on the distance meter – assuming of course that we stay alive until then.

3. We can measure the speed of a fundamental particle using a particle accelerator. However, measuring that speed without the accelerator or some similar device is impossible.

Just as science has its distinctive methodology, so does spirituality. Without using the spiritual methodology, we can gain some understanding of basic spiritual principles like the existence of soul and God using scientific means. However, to understand advanced spiritual principles, like the identity and personality of God, we need to adopt spiritual methods.

Srila Prabhupada inspired his scientist-followers to not only establish the basics of spirituality as scientific in the terms of modern science, but also to show how the entire process of Krishna consciousness was scientific, in the broad sense of the term "systematic, logical study of a subject." Subsequently, many ISKCON scientists like Dr T D Singh, Dr Michael Cremo and Dr Richard Thompson have written several books to fulfill the mandate given by Srila Prabhupada. By studying this wisdom and applying it in our life, we can experientially verify the truths taught therein, as the Bhagavad-gita (9.2) indicates.

Religion

Can We Be Spiritual Without Being Religious?

"I kept a distance from you because I'd thought that Hare Krishnas were religious. But now, after coming to know you better, I think you're spiritual." This was the remark of an old friend whom I'd met again after many years and whom I'd known before I was introduced to Krishna consciousness.

"Intriguing," I replied. "What made you think of us as religious, and what made you change your mind?"

"Well, you're so particular about your religious practices – a specific mantra, a specific God, a specific thing to wear, a specific institution to follow. All these things mark you as religious," he replied. "And religious people tend to be narrow-minded and fanatical. That's why I don't like them."

"But after talking with you, I saw that you are open-minded. You accept other religions as valid ways to God; that's a sign of your being spiritual. I like to meet spiritual people."

His parting remark made me ponder the idea of being 'spiritual-but-not-religious', a notion so popular that it has spawned a self-describing initialism SBNR: Is it really possible to be spiritual without being religious?

After thinking about it, this was my conclusion: Yes, if by 'spiritual' we imply open-mindedness and by 'religion' close-mindedness. No, if by 'spiritual' we refer to an elevated state of consciousness and by 'religious' a process to achieve that state of consciousness.

Let me explain.

The desire to be SBNR may be laudable, but its application is often questionable. Usually the intention is that we should be broad-minded, not narrow-minded. That intention is fine, but is the underlying implication valid? Is it true that spirituality makes us broad-minded and religion makes us narrow-minded?

These two terms "spiritual" and "religious" have so many connotations that without specifying their meaning, we can't say anything useful about either one. Let's focus on what these words normally connote in the context of being 'spiritual-not-religious': 'spiritual' usually refers to experience of the higher, deeper aspects of life, whereas 'religion' refers to adherence to certain beliefs and rituals given in a specific tradition. The implication is that spiritualists are open-minded because they are open to higher experience, regardless of how they come by that experience, while

Spirituality, a Higher Dimensional Science

religionists are close-minded because they stick only to what is given in their own religion and deride or dismiss other religions.

The Vedic wisdom-tradition points to an intriguing relationship between spirituality and religion. It explains that spirituality is meant to help us develop love for God. This is done through a harmonious combination of philosophy and religion, which constitute the two rails on which spirituality runs (please see the above figure). The philosophy aspect of spirituality involves study with the desire to understand matter, spirit, and the controller of both, God. And the religion aspect involves following certain rules and regulations that help us realize and directly experience higher spiritual truths.

These two aspects of spirituality are strikingly similar to the two aspects of modern science: the theoretical and the experimental. Science's theoretical aspect involves formulating hypotheses to explain the observable phenomena within the universe; it is similar to the philosophy aspect of spirituality. Science's experimental aspect involves following certain rules for regulating the laboratory environment so as to verify a given hypothesis; it is similar to the religion aspect of spirituality. Thus, spirituality can be considered a higher-dimensional science – higher-dimensional because it deals with a reality higher than that dealt with by material science.

Let's see how this understanding of spirituality as a combination of philosophy and religion illumines the SBNR issue.

Just as science requires some kind of experiment to be complete, spirituality requires some kind of religion to be complete. That is, spiritualists who want higher experiences need some process to consistently get those experiences. And that process can be identified as religion. So, to be spiritual, one would have to be religious in one way or another.

Does this imply that one can't be 'spiritual-not-religious'?

Literally yes, essentially no.

In essence the desire to be 'spiritual-not-religious' is the desire to be 'open-minded not close-minded.' The Vedic wisdom-tradition acknowledges that there are various ways to gain spiritual experiences, which culminate in the experience of love of God. The philosophy aspect of the tradition helps us to see the various great religions as authorized ways of progressing towards love of God. So, although it requires seekers to be religious if they want to be truly spiritual, it does not mandate close-mindedness. In fact, it encourages open-mindedness.

The Health Analogy

To understand this, let's extend the above comparison of spirituality with science by using the example of medical science. Therein, theory tells us what the healthy state is and what the diseased state is. And the experiments provide the means, the treatment, for moving from disease to health.

The Vedic wisdom-tradition tells us our present materialistic state of consciousness is a diseased one, referring to it as *bhava-roga*. It recommends various processes, like chanting the names of God, to take us back to our healthy spiritual state of consciousness, referring to these processes as *cikitsa*, treatment. The tradition is clear that the healthy spiritual state is not some vague misty feel-good experience; it is a steady state of being in which one loves God undistractedly. The diseased state is the state of loving anything other than God. Significantly, love of God is also the universally accepted common goal of the world's great theistic religions. Augustine, the Christian saint, puts it well in one of his prayers: "You have made us for you, and the heart never rests till it finds rest in you."

In this health analogy, the philosophy aspect of spirituality explains what the healthy spiritual level is and what the diseased material level is, while the religion aspect provides the means to rise from the diseased material level to the healthy spiritual level. Srila Prabhupada characterizes the inter-relationship of these two aspects: "Religion without philosophy is sentiment, or sometimes fanaticism, while philosophy without religion is mental speculation."

Let's take a closer look at the three parts of this statement:

1. **Religion without philosophy is sentiment:** When there is religion without philosophy, people don't have the intellectual framework to know what the actual spiritual level of consciousness is and to check whether they are factually experiencing it. So, they may stay sentimentally satisfied with whatever practices they have acquired from their present culture or past tradition, even if those practices don't actually make them spiritual. A common result of such sentimentalism is the naive acceptance of all ways as being more or less equal: "You have your way and I have mine. There are as many ways as there are people."

2. **Religion without philosophy is sometimes fanaticism:** Just as people can be healed by different treatments, people can become lovers of God by practicing different religions: Christianity, Islam, or Hinduism, for example.

The decisive test for a religion is whether it enables its followers to become spiritually healthy, to become lovers of God. In this light, religious fanatics are like narrow-minded proponents of a particular medical therapy who are ready to do away with all other therapies, being ready even to kill those taking and giving therapies that are not their own. Religious fanaticism is a titanic and tragic misunderstanding that arises from the lack of a proper philosophical understanding.

3. **Philosophy without religion is mental speculation**: The objective standard of love of God as the goal of religion enables us to choose among various religions just as we would choose between various medical treatments. But it doesn't make religion *per se* optional or dispensable. Without taking treatment, we will never become healthy. Similarly, without practicing religion, we will never develop love for God. The *Bhagavad-gita* (9.2) confirms that religion (*dharma*) brings about such realization (*pratyakshavagamam dharmyam*).

Many people merely read a lot of spiritual books, either as a hobby, being uncommitted spiritual explorers, or as a profession, being academic scholars. But they don't practice any religion. Consequently, they rarely realize, or experience as a reality, the subject they are reading about. By their refusal to practice any religion, they deprive themselves of such realization. So, their thoughts and talks about spirituality remain airy mental speculations without tangible connection with spiritual reality.

Often this kind of speculation ends in impersonalism,

the notion that the Absolute Truth is devoid of any personality, quality or activity. Why? Because as long as our intellectual endeavors to explore spirituality are not guided by scripture, we cannot get a clear understanding of the spiritual realm. So, by our speculation we basically negate the material and assume that when the negation is complete, what is left is spiritual. Srila Prabhupada pertinently points out, "Impersonalists always think backwards. They think that because there is form in matter, spirit should be formless...All these thoughts are basically material. To think either positively or negatively is still thinking materially." And again, "Negation does not mean negation of the positive. Negation of the nonessentials does not mean negation of the essential. Similarly, detachment from material forms does not mean nullifying the positive form."

Only when our intellectual endeavors are guided by scriptural revelation do we connect with the positive spiritual reality – Krishna's world of eternal love filled with activity, personality, variety, beauty and reciprocity.

What applies to 'philosophy-without-religion' also applies for SBNR If the advocates of SBNR deliberately avoid religion by not adopting any religious practices, then they will remain mental speculators. They may occasionally get experiences that they consider 'spiritual,' but they will usually gain no lasting transformation of heart and so will largely deprive themselves of enduring fulfillment in life.

However, if they want to avoid the close-minded mentality

associated with being religious, then they can adopt those religious practices that allow them to be open-minded about other religious practices. The practices of Krishna consciousness certainly encourages that open-mindedness. So, in accordance with the open-minded intent of the usage, Krishna-devotees can indeed be 'spiritual-not-religious.' At the same time, in terms of content , a more complete understanding is that devotees are both spiritual and religious.

Is Institutionalization Anti-spiritual?

Conceptual analysis apart, many SBNR proponents argue that anything affiliated with an institution automatically becomes a religion and can't be classified as spiritual. Why? Because, they claim, that institutionalization chokes the essence of spirituality.

While this is definitely a possibility, it is by no means an absolute necessity. In fact, without institutionalization, spirituality will not be able to share its spirit with society and so won't be able to benefit people at large.

Let's understand this with an analogy. The purpose of spirituality is the development of love of God. If we compare the flow of our heart's love towards God to the flow of a river towards the ocean, then the institution is like the river bed.

If there is no river bed, only those rivers that have an exceptionally strong flow will reach the ocean. Rivers with a weak flow will, when faced with obstacles, stagnate and dry up. Similarly, if there is no institutional support, only those people who have an extraordinary spiritual urge will attain love for God. Those with average spiritual urge will, when faced with obstacles, stagnate and give up.

Just as several gently-flowing tributaries unite to comprise a forcefully-flowing river, several people with average spiritual urge unite to generate an above-average spiritual current that carries all of them forward swiftly. Just as a forceful river shapes a bed for itself as it keeps flowing, these people organize the necessities and facilities for their steady and smooth spiritual progress. Over time, this organized infrastructure takes the form of a spiritual institution.

Just as a river may be dammed by self-interested individuals, a spiritual institution may be damned by materially-minded people who are interested more in appropriating its facilities than in actualizing its purpose. To prevent such misuse, spiritual institutions need to have:

1. Systematic philosophical education so that its members become instinctively self-aware that their destination is not the dam (material aggrandizement) but the ocean (non-material devotional enrichment)

2. Regular religious practices so as to generate a powerful spiritual current that either exposes the materialism of self-seeking people, thereby pushing them to the sidelines, or purifies them of their materialism, thereby pulling them into its onward flow.

Some people may presume that they don't need any institution because their spiritual urge is strong enough for a solo journey. However, they usually underestimate the materialistic tug of their surroundings and overestimate their own resistance power. Consequently, their spiritual progress tends to be at best sporadic, being at the mercy of their unpredictable inner moods and uncontrollable outer circumstances. If they can just summon the humility to acknowledge that their solo trip is becoming more of a camp than a journey, then they will see the wisdom of joining those who are steadily on the move. And just in case these seekers are among the rare few who are genuinely self-motivated, then by joining an authentic spiritual institution, they will be able to guide and inspire other less self-motivated spiritual seekers.

So, vigilant institutionalization is essential to make spirituality accessible and beneficial to society at large.

Inner vigilance amidst institutionalization

Nonetheless, many concerns of the 'spiritual-but-not-religious' proponents are valid even for us as devotees. We need to guard against complacency, wherein we assume that just joining an institution automatically makes us spiritually advanced. Each one of us has to take individual responsibility for our spiritual advancement. Just as avoidance of commitments to external practices can be a kind of spiritual irresponsibility for the SBNR people , the mere adherence of external practices without due attention to our inner development can be a form of spiritual irresponsibility for us.

The scriptures caution us about this pitfall by underscoring that the purpose of all our religious activities should be the remembrance of Krishna, as is proclaimed in an oft-quoted verse from the Padma Purana:

smartavyah satatam vishnur vismartavyo na jatucit
sarve vidhi-nishedhah syur etayor eva kinkarah

"Always remember Vishnu; never forget him. All the rules and prohibitions mentioned in the scriptures are the servants of these two principles."

By thus simultaneously adhering to external practices and internally cultivating remembrance of Krishna, we can avoid the pitfalls that alarm the 'spiritual-but-not-religious' advocates and make authentic, swift, sustained spiritual advancement towards life's ultimate goal of developing love for Krishna.

To conclude, Krishna consciousness embraces the intent of open-mindedness underlying the SNBR idea: it acknowledges the reality and validity of other paths, and also focuses on an inner transformation that culminates in the supreme fulfillment of love for God. At the same time, Krishna consciousness rejects the SBNR content of uncommitted feel-good exploration: it emphasizes that to experience a real and tangible transformation that lasts, one needs to adopt a specific path and follow it diligently .

Conversion to What: Intolerance or Transcendence?

This article is a compilation of several conversations between Hindu intellectuals (HI) and ISKCON scholars (IS) on many different occasions. To cover the various issues in a systematic way, those conversations are presented here as one, continuous conversation between two non-historical individuals.

HI: An issue of great concern, even alarm, for the culture of India is the rampant conversion done by Christian missionaries.

IS: Let's understand this issue of conversion from a broader philosophical perspective. The goal of all religions – including Christianity – is to help people develop love of God, to convert people from being materialists to becoming spiritualists.

But different people approach God for different motives, which the Vaishnava saint-scholar Bhaktivinoda Thakura has categorized into four major levels: fear, desire, duty and love.

1. Fear:

Some people fear, "If I disobey God, then he may punish me for my wrongdoings. So better let me go to his temple and pacify him by my worship." This sort of worship is certainly better than atheism, but it is based on a very limited and a somewhat negative conception of God as a stern judge, as a cosmic punisher – not as an object of love.

2. Desire:

Some people think, "There are so many things I want; if I pray to God, perhaps He will give them to me." Here the conception of God is more positive, as a potent desire-fulfiller. But still the relationship with him is utilitarian, based on give-and-take rather than love.

3. Duty:

Some people reason, "God has already given me so much – life, body, health, food, clothing, shelter. It is my duty to go periodically to His temple and thank him." Here the relationship is based on gratitude for what has already been given and not on greed for what one wants to receive. So it is a somewhat steady relationship. However, duty can over time become a burden. Moreover, the focus in this level is still on what God has done for me, not on God himself.

4. Love:

This is the purest level of approaching God, where a devotee feels, "My dear Lord, you are the supreme object of my love; I have been offering my love to so many people and things, but that has never made me happy. Now I simply want to love and serve you eternally and I do not want anything worldly in return for my service; I simply wish to love you and to be loved by you. Just as a parent takes care of the child without the child having to ask them for anything, I know that you will similarly take care of me. I will accept whatever is your plan for me and keep serving you no matter what happens in life."

Conversions are fruitful only if they raise a person's level of approaching God by offering deep spiritual understanding or experience. Modern Christianity operates largely on the platforms of fear and desire – despite the fact that Jesus explicitly emphasized the commandment to love God as the supreme commandment. It appears to many observers that the conversions done by Christian missionaries today are primarily on the same two levels – fear of eternal damnation and desire for material gain. More often than not, all that happens by such materially-motivated conversions is that the converts change from being Hindu materialists to becoming Christian materialists.

HI: But this conversion often makes a huge difference to the convert's attitude toward his original culture. Whereas he was earlier appreciative of – or at least neutral to –Indian culture, he now becomes hostile to it. And often this hostility is fostered by some Christian missionaries who decry Indic rituals and traditions as demoniac. Sometimes the convert has to "prove" his conversion by publicly disowning his past forms of worship, by breaking or burning the pictures of Hindu gods or even spitting or stamping on them.

IS: Such fanaticism is heartbreaking to even hear about, what to speak of endure....To place this in proper perspective, let's discuss the three categories into which modern thinkers have classified the various religious paths: exclusivist, pluralist and inclusivist.

Followers of the exclusivist path claim that their way is the only exclusive way to God. They further claim that all those who don't accept their path are destined to go to hell – forever. So they become intolerant to all other paths and believe that they are "saving" people by converting them to their path, no matter what the means. Religious exclusivity sometimes degenerates into fundamentalist violence. This further puts off intelligent people, who are already skeptical of the claim to exclusivity. After all, if God is unlimited, why should one particular religion have monopoly on the path to God?

HI (nodding): Most Christian missionaries are highly exclusivist. Hindu culture, on the other hand, has historically been more broad-minded.

IS: Yes. The second category is pluralism. Pluralism is the notion that there are many paths to God. Nowadays, this notion is sometimes expanded to say that there are as many paths to God as there are people. While this notion seems to promote religious tolerance, it often breeds spiritual impotence.

HI (startled): Impotence?

IS: A religious system can be compared to a university meant to train students in knowledge and love of God. The claim to exclusivism is like the claim of a medical student that his college is the only college that can produce doctors. This is obviously a fanatical and fallacious claim. The claim to pluralism, on the other hand, is like the claim that any building anywhere can produce doctors. In the name of pluralism, Hinduism today has become such a hodgepodge that most Hindus today have very little idea of what paths and goals their scriptures teach. Consequently, when confronted with Christian missionary criticism of Hinduism, many Hindus are unable to defend their beliefs and practices.

HI (thoughtfully): I had never thought of the effects of pluralism in that way ... I can't say that I agree entirely with what you say; I will have to think about it...But what was the third category you mentioned?

IS: Inclusivism. This teaches that there are not many paths, but basically one path with many levels on it. The path to become a doctor is essentially one: to study the medical subjects and learn the relevant skills. There may be different universities to teach medicine and they may teach in slightly different ways, but that doesn't mean we unthinkingly accept every building everywhere as a medical college. Unfortunately, this – an uncritical acceptance of all paths – is what has happened in India. Consequently, although religion is a big part of life in India, it has largely become reduced to a social and cultural affair that provides a break from the daily routine and has become devoid of spiritual potency.

HI: What exactly do you mean by spiritual potency?

IS: Spiritual potency of religion means its ability to deliver non-material or spiritual happiness. The Srimad Bhagavatam declares *bhakti pareshanubhava viraktir anyatra ca* (11.2.42) "Bhakti delivers experience of the transcendental Supreme Lord, an experience which is so satisfying, so enriching that it makes one detached from all other experiences." The ultimate purpose of all religion is to enable people to experience the divine happiness of loving God and thus become detached from selfish, materialistic pleasures. The Vedic scriptures give clear, specific and powerful practices to help us experience this spiritual happiness. But when all paths are considered equal without evaluating their effects, then the potent Vedic path gets obscured in a medley of diluted and perverted paths. Consequently, many Indians, who follow one of these pseudo-religious paths, experience hardly any deep, spiritual happiness. So, when they are tempted to follow another path that offers tangible material benefits, they see no reason to desist.

HI: Interesting. In connection with our discussion on three categories of paths, I want to point out a peculiar feature of Indian "secularism". Despite the overtly exclusivist claims of Christian missionaries, the Indian government and media pamper them in the name of secularism. Secularism should basically imply governmental impartiality toward all religions. In countries like USA, secularism means that minority-religions get the freedom to practice their beliefs and they democratically get a voice in the polity according to their sizes. And the majority-religion in USA – protestant Christianity – gets a respectable place and influence according to its electoral strength. But in India, due to vote bank politics, secularism is abused to provide special facilitation for minority-religions and impose special restriction on the majority religion. For example, today, in India, legally it is far easier to start a Christian church or a Christian missionary school then it is to start a Hindu temple or a Hindu missionary school. Or, here's an even more egregious example: when Muslims want to go for Haj, the government makes special arrangements and even subsidizes their pilgrimage fare. But when Hindus want to go on pilgrimage to Badrinath, the government offers no such facility.

What makes the whole issue worse is the prejudiced media portrayal by the western media and the westernized Indian media. Historically, few countries have been as hospitable to other cultures as India, thanks to the Hindu culture of welcoming and respecting guests as representatives of God. For example,

- India is the country that gave asylum to the Christians who were persecuted in Syria in Antioch and Damascus even in the fourth century. They have been living here peacefully till this date.

- India gave asylum to the Persians when they had to flee Persia due to fear of the Arabian invaders. These Zoroastrians who took asylum in the Gujarat area are all leading prosperous and fearless lives till this date.

- When the Jews sought asylum in India after being driven out of their land, they were taken care of by India. This was not the case with several countries in the West where the Jews were persecuted.

- After the conquest of Tibet by China, the persecuted Buddhists under the Dalai Lama were generously accommodated by India in McLeod Ganja in Himachal Pradesh, where they live peacefully even today.

So, minorities have always been given protection and facility to live in India, thanks to the Hindu ethos of tolerance. But when Hindus try to protect their legitimate interests from the extreme and fundamentalist activities of some Christian missionaries, the media immediately brands the tolerant Hindus as intolerant and the fundamentalist minorities as helpless victims. It is sad that these situations have led to violent conflicts; violence in the name of religion is unfortunate and regrettable. But the sponsoring of culturally-destructive conversion is a form of extremism that inflames violence on both sides. It is high time that the media set the record straight by reporting both sides of the story fairly.

IS: The foundational problem is the intellectual lethargy of Indians in understanding their own national legacy. Indians don't protest against attacks on their culture because they don't realize the value of what they are losing. In academic studies of religion, there is the concept of religious capital, which refers to the degree of mastery of and attachment to a particular religious culture. Businesspeople may readily give up their present business if they have not invested much capital in it, if they are not getting much returns out of it and if a new business offers better prospects. Similarly, person will change their religion – their religious business – if they have not invested much thoughts and emotions into it (their capital), if they are not getting an understanding of life or a sense of peace, joy and belonging by it (their returns) and if they get material benefits by changing to another religion (their better prospects). So it is important for Indian spiritual leaders to create religious capital among Indians by giving them spiritual knowledge and experience. Otherwise, most Indians will not oppose conversion or, worse still, may even get converted themselves for better material prospects.

HI: Well, frequently the idea of better prospects is just a sham. Though the sufferings of lower caste Hindus due to caste-based discrimination are real and deplorable, getting converted doesn't really solve their problem. They often find themselves treated as second-grade members of the religion to which they have converted.

Some missionaries claim to be faith-healers and proclaim that they can cure all those who convert. Many sick Hindu peasants, being unable to afford medical expenses, get lured, but the magic healing never happens. Their suffering only gets compounded: due to the delay in taking medical treatment, their disease worsens, thus necessitating further expenditure. And they simultaneously undergo wrenching mental trauma and social alienation due to the whole conversion melodrama. Many such incidents are described the documentary *Bad Manna* by the Scandinavian Pia Skov, who, significantly, is herself a Christian disillusioned with the missionary malpractices.

IS: Such practices are certainly devious. And they underscore what I was saying earlier: the urgent necessity for philosophical education among Indians. You see, many people have a primitive, tribal "we-they" mindset. They see existence as a perpetual battle between "we" versus "they", where "they" refers to their rivals or enemies. When religious zeal becomes superimposed on this tribal mentality, then the battle takes the form of "the good we" versus "the evil they", where "they" includes all those who don't follow "our true religion". Once religious conversion gets rationalized as a battle against evil, or perhaps a "saving" from the evil, then the missionaries become blinded to their own evil deeds, for they feel their "noble" ends justify any means – no matter how evil.

Sometimes, Hindus may also succumb to the same "we-they" mindset in reverse, where all Christians become "the evil they". To save us from this tribal mindset, the Vedic scriptures teach a profound and practical philosophy that engenders universal consciousness. They state that all living beings are the beloved children of one God and so, spiritually, we are all one family, as celebrated in the famous Vedic aphorism *vasudhaiva kutumbakam*. The Vedic texts proclaim that all people are intrinsically, spiritually good. If they are presently acting in evil ways, that is due to the illusion that covers their spiritual goodness. The Vedic texts further supply us rational, objective parameters to assess the extent of the illusion that covers a person. Equipped with these parameters, we can objectively categorize people without falling prey to the "we-they" mindset.

HI (thoughtfully): This "we-they" mentality you are talking about is a deep point... What are the rational parameters by which people are categorized?

IS: The Bhagavad-gita analyzes all material existence in terms of the three modes of material nature: mode of goodness (sattva-guna), mode of passion (rajo-guna) and mode of ignorance (tamo-guna). The modes are subtle, psychic forces that shape the interaction between consciousness and matter. Those affected by the mode of goodness are characterized by knowledge, thoughtfulness and satisfaction; those affected by the mode of passion, by cravings for pleasure, power and prestige; and those affected by the mode of ignorance, by laziness, intoxication and violence. Higher than all these three modes is transcendence, where people can see, with enlightened vision, their loving relationship with all living beings. The more people are infected by passion and ignorance, the more they act in evil ways that harm themselves and others. The more they are permeated by goodness and transcendence, the more they act in good ways that uplift themselves and others.

Note how the Vedic classification is not based on any religious labels, but is based on objective criterion and has universal application. Now, Christians, like all other human beings, are situated across the spectrum of these three modes; some in goodness, some in passion and some in ignorance. According to this analysis, the devious conversion tactics are used by Christians in the lower modes of passion and ignorance. And just as we find these devious tactics distasteful, so do Christians in the mode of goodness. That's why even some Christians have expressed concern over the means used to convert people.

HI (catching on): I had heard of the modes earlier, but had never thought that they could be applied to this way. Not only are such conversions done by those in the lower modes, but they are also targeted at those in the modes of passion and ignorance, who don't care to discern spiritual truth on one hand and who want quick material gains on the other.

IS (nodding): Yes. But such conversions don't do anything to change the modes of a person. Various religions are essentially like different universities meant to change people's qualities from evil to good. Just as an engineering student does not become an engineer merely by entering into a college, no person becomes "saved" just by stamping himself as belonging to a particular religion. They will be saved only when they diligently practice the spiritual disciplines taught by their religion, and change their qualities and desires. Unfortunately, superficial religionists, not understanding or practicing the essence of their own religion, imagine that they are "saving" others from evil by converting them, while they are yet to save themselves from the evil qualities that have gripped them.

HI (wryly): I think we have to pray: may God save India from these "saviors"!

IS: But God has given us the means to save ourselves and everyone else – Indians and non-Indians alike.

HI: What is that means?

IS: The spiritual philosophy given in the Vedic scriptures is so comprehensive, coherent and cogent that it can withstand and counter all possible criticisms and dialectically establish itself as offering the best understanding of life and its purpose. And the Vedic spiritual practices like chanting of the holy names can easily and effectively give people a taste of transcendence by which they will no longer be attracted by cheap material allurements. We need to systematically and vigorously share the Vedic principles and practices with as many people as possible. In fact, Srila Prabhupada did exactly that – and was able to attract thousands of people from all over the world to follow Vedic culture.

HI: Yes, I have seen that ISKCON has a lot of foreign devotees.

It's almost like ISKCON is doing a reverse-conversion by getting Western people from Christian and other backgrounds to adopt Indian culture.

IS: Yes, but this conversion is a conversion that goes far beyond the change of religious denomination, cultural lifestyle or social affiliation. It is a fundamental change of consciousness, a change of core desires and ambitions from material to spiritual, a change from being a selfish exploiter to becoming a selfless servant of God and all His children. And this change doesn't engender disrespect of one's earlier tradition. Srila Prabhupada declared that Jesus Christ was our guru because he had so much love for God that he laid down his life for the sake of God. Whenever Srila Prabhupada met dedicated Christians, he didn't try to convert them; he encouraged them to follow the Bible faithfully, and strive to develop genuine love for God. Those people who had been nominal Christians earlier and who accepted the Vedic wisdom-tradition did so because they found herein a potent process for developing love of God authentically and swiftly.

And developing love of God is the change that all religions – including Christianity – are ultimately meant to bring about. Indeed, this is the only change that can bring real, lasting happiness, individually and collectively. People are being increasingly plundered of this wealth of inner happiness, by the common enemy of all religions: atheistic materialism. That's why, in the 1950s Srila Prabhupada made a fervent appeal for united action to the leaders of the world's religions: 'Hindus, Muslims, Christians, and the members of the other sects that have convincing faith in the authority of God must not sit idly now and silently watch the rapid growth of a Godless civilization. There is the supreme will of God, and no nation or society can live in peace and prosperity without acceptance of this vital truth.'

It is tragic when religionists instead of benefitting materialistic people who are living without any God consciousness dissipate their energies in deriding the beliefs and practices of other religions, and converting them. This situation is like allopathic doctors instead of treating sick patients dissipate their energies in deriding Ayurvedic medicine and trying to drag patients from an Ayurvedic hospital to an allopathic hospital.

HI: Yes, this example hits the nail on the head... We Hindus must also do our part in pre-empting the social, cultural and economic factors that make people vulnerable to conversion. We can no longer stay caught in caste discrimination; we need to set up effective systems for taking care of impoverished Hindus; we need to unite all fellow-Hindus on the basis of the principles of dharma. Then we can counter the menace of conversion.

IS: Yes. It is terrible when those who are receptive to Vedic culture become hostile due to the misconceptions propagated by narrow-minded missionaries ignorant of the essential purpose of religion. Srila Prabhupada, the founder-acharya of ISKCON, emphasized that Hindus are better situated than those following other religions because they are within the house of the Vedas. This implies that they have lesser cultural and conceptual barriers blocking them from adopting the process by which they can most easily and expeditiously attain love of God.

The more we can offer spiritual education to people, the more they will understand the essential purpose of religion. Then they will see for themselves the absurdity and the tragedy of such conversions. And more importantly, they will become empowered to attain genuine devotion for God. Such an intellectually-inspired respiritualization of Indian society and of the global society at large will make a real difference in the world.

Extremist misconceptions about the Bhagavad-gita

Over the last few weeks due to the abortive attempt in Russia to ban the Gita as an extremist book, the question came up repeatedly on Google as well as in the media: "Is the Gita an extremist book?" On looking at the many voices that opposed the "extremist" labeling, I found that most of the voices that defended the Gita, though well-meaning, appealed only to respect for cultural and religious sentiments and for freedom of speech – and lacked intellectual depth. Consequently, I felt driven to prepare an article that presents the traditional devotional understanding of the Gita with sensitivity to contemporary intellectual concerns. Such an article, I felt, would not only address the limited, time-specific "extremist" accusations against the Gita, but also serve a more enduring and universal purpose of offering a glimpse into the profundity of its wisdom. So here we go.

A Message of Love

The Bhagavad-gita, far from being an extremist book, is a book of wisdom and a message of love. It reveals divinity's love for humanity; it is only our extreme disorientation from divine love that makes us imagine that the Gita is an extremist literature.

Let us first understand the Gita's essential message of love and then analyze some of its aspects that may seem to belie this message and may, if taken totally out of context and wildly misinterpreted, be seen as extremist.

Krishna starts His message of love by enlightening Arjuna: we are all souls, spiritual beings (Gita 2.13), entitled to rejoice in eternal love with the supremely lovable and loving God, Krishna. All of us long for lasting love, but we seek it on the material platform that is inherently fleeting. The Gita's philosophical wisdom of our eternal spiritual identity creates a lasting foundation on which we can build an edifice of love that the storms of time will never bring crumbling down.

In the Gita, Krishna offers a concise overview of the various paths for spiritual progress – karma-yoga (the path of detached action), jnana-yoga (the path of analysis), dhyana-yoga (the path of meditation) and bhakti-yoga (the path of love). Simultaneously throughout the Gita (2.61, 3.30, 4.3, 5.29, 6.30, 7.1, 8.14, 9.26-27, 10.9-12, 11.53-54, 12.6-7, 13.18, 14.27, 15.19, 16.5, 17.26-27, 18.64-66), he hints, indicates, states, asserts and proclaims that the path of love is the best path. As the Gita progresses, the hints become more and more explicit; the secret secret becomes an increasingly open secret till its emotional climax at its end (18.64-66), where Krishna bares his heart's love in a disarming proclamation of love and an endearing call for love.

Thus, the Gita is essentially a revelation of divinity's love for humanity as well as a love call for humanity's reciprocal love for divinity.

Potential Misunderstandings about the Gita

Let us now look at three aspects of the Gita that are at times misunderstood.

A.   The Battlefield Setting of the Bhagavad-gita

The Bhagavad-gita is sometimes misunderstood as calling for violence due to its battlefield setting. However, the Gita uses that setting to demonstrate that its call for transcendence is practical, responsible and dynamic. Let's see how the setting serves these three purposes:

1. **The practicality of spirituality:** Many people feel that spirituality is too other-worldly and so is impractical or irrelevant given the urgent practical demands of this world. To address their concern, the Bhagavad-gita's spiritual message is delivered on a setting that is eminently this-worldly and calls for the most urgent practical action: a battlefield. By showing how its spiritual wisdom solaced and empowered a responsible head of state, Arjuna, who broke down on a battlefield, the Gita illustrates poignantly the universal applicability of its teachings. If a person on a battlefield spared time for gaining its spiritual wisdom and found it relevant, practical and empowering, then no one needs to doubt the practicality of the Gita's message. And no circumstance needs to warrant relegating the study of the Gita's message to the "to be done later" category.

2. **The social responsibility of spiritualists:** While the Bhagavad-gita offers a message that can guide any individual in any circumstance to personal transcendence, peace and fulfillment, it also recognizes that people at large can benefit from its message only when the prevailing sociopolitical order fosters moral and spiritual integrity. When the ruling heads of state are morally and spiritually depraved, as they were before the Kurushetra war, assertive action is essential to prevent people from being exploited, abused and ruined. The Mahabharata sections preceding the narration of the Gita describe vividly

    a. The multiple injustices and atrocities committed by

the ruling heads of state, the Kauravas

b.   The repeated efforts of the victims, the Pandavas, to restore justice and morality in a peaceful way

c.   The utter disdain with which the Kauravas rejected all the attempts for peace, thus making a peaceful solution impossible

For those victimized by massive injustice, the Gita doesn't condone a passive spectator role that reduces noble pacifism to impotent and suicidal utopianism. Instead, the Gita advocates pragmatic assertive action for protecting basic human rights. That violence should be the last expression of such assertiveness – and never anything other than the last – is illustrated by the exhaustive peace efforts that preceded it. The very fact that several globally acclaimed champions of non-violence like Mahatma Gandhi found inspiration in the message of the Gita demonstrates that violence is not its core message. Of course, those who find the battlefield setting discomforting have tried to explain it (away) in metaphorical terms, but such an explanation undoes the intrinsic pragmatism that makes the Gita's message of transcendence so appealing. By delivering this message on a battlefield, the Gita illustrates that even those who consider life's ultimate goals to be other-worldly have a this-worldly responsibility to contribute to establishing and protecting the moral and spiritual fabric of society.

3.   **The inner dynamics of spirituality:** The metaphorical interpretation of the Gita's setting is not wrong, but it best

harmonizes with the overall spirit of the Gita when seen as a supplement to –and not a substitute for – its historical context. Then, the battlefield setting, in addition to its historicity, represents our internal consciousness that features the battle between godly desires and ungodly desires. Each of us needs to win this inner battle if we are to play our part in establishing moral and spiritual integrity in society and not let our ungodly attachments to selfish interests sabotage our godly aspirations for personal integrity. Even when our godly aspirations are outnumbered by our ungodly attachments, as was the case with the godly Pandavas fighting the ungodly Kauravas, the Gita's setting conveys the morale-boosting reassurance that when we harmonize our godly desires with God's will, then his supreme power will empower us to attain inner victory and self-mastery.

To summarize, the Gita's battlefield setting, when seen in its historical and philosophical context, reveals itself to be a call not for blanket violence, but for thoroughgoing spiritual activism.

B.   The Vision of God as Destroyer:

The eleventh chapter of the Gita describes the universal form of God which emits blazing flames of destruction and devours all directions. Though such a conception of God may seem brutal and ghastly, it underpins a subtle but essential truth: the destruction and death that inevitably characterize the world are not outside the jurisdiction of God. God is not primarily the destroyer, but the restorer; when the temporary stands in the way of the eternal, as it does for all of us who are infatuated with the temporary and neglectful of the eternal, God destroys the temporary to make way for the eternal. Moreover, a careful reading of the full eleventh chapter reveals its essential import. Arjuna asks to see the universal form of God, becomes terrified on seeing the destruction therein and immediately changes his mind asking to be shown the beautiful two-handed form of Krishna once again. Just as the destructiveness of the universal form serves to re-direct Arjuna to the beauty of Krishna, similarly, the Gita teaches us, that the destruction and death that beset the world can serve to re-direct our heart to the eternality and the beauty of Krishna.

C.   Blunt Value Judgments

Some of us may be disturbed when we encounter in the Bhagavad-gita words that indicate strong value judgments: fool (mudha: 7.25), lowest among human beings (naradhama: 16.17) and so forth. To gain a proper understanding of why they are used, we need to contextualize them philosophically.

Philosophical contextualization

Value judgments emerge from values, which in turn grow out of a philosophy. If we go beyond the value judgments to the values and the philosophy, we will often find that the philosophy has a sense of its own. And once we understand the philosophy, we will find that its resulting values are not so different from our own. Then, with this intellectual framework in place, the value judgments will become at least intelligible, even if not acceptable. In other words, we need to judge the values before we judge the value judgments.

Let's therefore look beyond the value judgments to the values and the philosophy of the Bhagavad-gita.

The Gita (14.4) advocates a remarkably ecumenical worldview in which God accepts as his own children all living beings – not just humans, but even animals and plants. Only recently and nascently has our political correctness started waking us up to animal rights. But thousands of years ago, the Gita confers upon all subhuman beings (or the more politically correct "nonhuman beings") the spiritual right of integral and eternal membership in the family of God.

Further, the Gita (4.7-9) describes that God so loves all his children that he personally descends to this world –not just once, but periodically again and again and yet again.

Moreover, the Gita (9.32-33) by its universal and accessible gospel of devotion opens the doors of redemption for one and all, irrespective of caste, gender or other such worldly designations.

This universality and accessibility of the Gita's message has been appreciated by many eminent thinkers. Here's Aldous Huxley's quote as an example: "The Bhagavad-Gita is the most systematic statement of spiritual evolution of endowing value to mankind... its enduring value is subject not only to India but to all of humanity."

We may wonder: if the Gita advocates such lofty values, then why does it hand out blunt value judgments?

Open-minded, but not empty-minded

The Bhagavad-gita presents an open-minded worldview that integrates all people, no matter how diverse their values, goals and paths. According to their level of spiritual evolution, the Gita assigns them an appropriate position on a universal continuum that extends downwards to total spiritual ignorance and upwards to complete spiritual realization. The Gita also offers them versions of spirituality customized to their levels so as to inspire and facilitate them to rise higher on the spiritual continuum.

The Gita is broad-minded, but not empty-minded; it does not imagine vacuously that all levels on the spiritual continuum are the same. That's why the Gita (16.7-20) disapproves unequivocally mindsets and lifestyles that violate one's spiritual integrity and propel one downwards on the spiritual continuum.

The Gita considers godlessness not as an intrinsic quality of the soul, but as an extrinsic infection acquired by unwholesome contact. According to the Gita, godlessness is a sickness for the soul, a sickness that is easily and thoroughly curable by the therapy of devotional service. The Gita doesn't equate a mortally sick person with that of a vibrantly healthy person, for that would condemn the sick person to perpetual sickness and distort laudable open-mindedness into deplorable empty-mindedness.

Its value-judgments are like the exasperated outbursts of a caring doctor dealing with a suffering patient who stubbornly refuses to take the treatment.

Seen in this light, the Gita's value judgments are not expressions of condemnation, but of compassion. The Gita uses strong judgmental words like fools. Srila Prabhupada as the pre-eminent modern-day Gita exponent was known to use the word "rascal" quite often, but his use follows in the compassionate – not condemnatory – spirit of Krishna, as is evident from the following quote, "The only concern of the devotees is that so many rascals are suffering in the concocted civilization of illusory sense enjoyment, how can they be saved? So our Krishna Consciousness movement is made for that saving the rascals."

Fathoming by Tuning

Perhaps it is fitting to sign off with an apt quote of the Austrian philosopher Rudolph Steiner, "In order to approach a creation as sublime as the Bhagavad-Gita with full understanding it is necessary to attune our soul to it." Attuning our soul to the Gita can be best done by understanding the Gita from those who have tuned their soul to it and are living its essential message. A prime example of a Gita teacher who was first and foremost a Gita liver and a Gita lover was Srila Prabhupada. His translation and commentary on the Gita, Bhagavad Gita As It Is, is not only the most widely distributed and read English commentary of the Gita, but is also the Gita commentary that has brought about the most transformative effect among its readers. By understanding the Gita from Gita lovers like him, we can not only dispel "extremist" misunderstandings about the Gita, but, more importantly, can also acquire essential understanding of the Gita.

To conclude, while it is certainly important to defend the Gita so as to prevent it from being banned officially in any part of the world, it is equally, if not more, important to understand the Gita so that we don't ban it unofficially in our own lives by mistaking it to be incomprehensible or irrelevant.

Question: Can the Bhagavad-gita be seen metaphorically?

Answer: The metaphorical interpretation of scripture has a long and respected history within the Vedic tradition. It was integral to a method of scriptural interpretation known as *gauna vrtti* (secondary meaning) as contrasted with *mukhya vrtti* (primary meaning) and was reserved for the special contexts like those where:

1. **The direct meaning would result in obvious absurdities**: The standard example for this in Indian philosophy is the sentence "His house is on the river." As no house can lie on the river, this has to be interpreted as meaning "his house is on the banks of the river."

2. **The direct meaning could be supplemented – but not supplanted – with an additional meaning obtained by looking at the implied symbolism:** Here are a few examples of the use of this approach by eminent Vedic teachers:

    *   Sripad Madhvacharya in his well-known analysis of the Mahabharata, the Mahabharata Tatparya Nirnaya, states that the Itihasas like the Mahabharata and the Ramayana can be understood at three levels:

    *   The literal: The events described in these literature happened historically as they were described,

    *   The ethical: These historical events serve as moral benchmarks to guide us in our present-day ethical decision-making.

    *   The metaphorical: These historical events symbolize truths relevant to seekers on the spiritual path.

    Madhvacharya is quick to emphasize that the literal understanding is the most accurate and the other understandings are only to gain additional, esoteric insight that is consistent with – and not contradictory to – the literal understanding.

- Sri Vedanta Deshika, a prominent teacher in the line of Ramanujacharya, used the metaphorical understanding of the kidnapping of Sita in the Ramayana to show how that traumatic event is relevant to us now: "When the soul represented by Sita turns away from God represented by Lord Rama, the mind represented by Ravana immediately carries the soul away from God and imprisons it in the body represented by Lanka."

- Srila Bhaktivinoda Thakura, a prominent author-teacher in the Vaishnava tradition, used this approach in his Krishna Samhita (Chapters 4-6) and also Chaitanya Shikshamrita (Part 5, Chapter 6) to explain how the various demons killed by Krishna in Vrindavana represent the various anarthas (undesirable behavioral traits) that the seeker needs to eradicate from his heart, which is like Vrindavana. Bhaktivinoda Thakura doesn't deny the literal or historical reality of Krishna's demon-killing pastimes; these pastimes occurred in the past when Krishna had descended to the world. But he also states that the killing of the demons by Krishna also represents the destruction of the anarthas in our heart by Krishna that will happen when we hear those demon-killing pastimes submissively.

- Srila Prabhupada himself used the metaphorical interpretation of the Kurukshetra war occasionally, as in his talk while giving initiations for the first time in America in 1966 at New York, as quoted in *The Hare Krishna Explosion* by Hayagriva Dasa.

"Krishna and Arjuna sat in the same chariot. But Arjuna knew that Krishna is the Supreme. We are also in a kind of chariot with Krishna. That chariot is this material body, and within the heart Lord Krishna is present as the Supersoul, witnessing all our activities. Even though He accompanies us within the material world, Krishna is never attached." Paraphrasing Srila Prabhupada, the author further writes, "He then reminds us that we should never fret when confronted with adversities, for we should always know that Lord Krishna is driving our chariot."

Srila Prabhupada rejected time and again the metaphorical interpretation of the Kurukshetra war when it was used as a substitute for the literal interpretation, as a means to deny the historicity of the Mahabharata war, as a tool to explain away into non-occurrence the violence that occurred there.

Is the Ramayana relevant today?

"The Ramayana comprises stories from ancient times. Is it practically relevant today?" When I was asked this question in the midst of the rush of the recent Rama Navmi festival, I answered briefly, stating that though its stories may be from an ancient setting, they embody timeless values that are relevant to us even today. I also told the questioner that I would write an article explaining how they are relevant. Here is that article.

From "me" to "we"

One of the primary values that it conveys – selfless sacrifice – is especially relevant in our present times where people are becoming increasingly enamored by self-seeking lifestyles. Contemporary culture largely glamorizes the "me" paradigm, which impels people to seek their personal gratification without caring about its cost for others. When the same inconsiderate individualism causes us to neglect or manipulate the people around us – our family members, our neighbors and colleagues, then it boomerangs to wound our heart, afflicting it with emotional ruptures and gnawing loneliness. Thus, the "me" paradigm, despite its instinctive appeal to our ego, is disastrously myopic.

If we wish to have more satisfying and sustainable relationships, we need to rise from this myopic "me" paradigm to the holistic "we" paradigm. As this paradigm shift can be challenging, it is helpful, even essential, to have inspiring role models and narratives to draw from. For mining such inspiration, the Ramayana serves as an inexhaustible mother lode; it offers us a panorama of jewel-like personalities who embody the spirit of sacrifice in various poignant real-life situations:

1. The example of Rama's sacrifice in accepting the sentence of exile despite having committed no fault just to preserve the word of honor of his father, king Dasharatha, points the way to bridging the ever-expanding parent-children generation gaps.

2. The example of Sita's sacrifice in preferring the dangers of the forest to the security of the palace offers a stirring example of valuing the marital bond that has become much devalued due to an increasingly casual approach to sexuality and matrimony.

3. The example of Lakshmana's sacrifice in choosing to stand unflinchingly by the side of his elder brother during the latter's hour of crisis and thereby gaining a profound mutually enriching bond can serve as an antidote for the superficial relationships that characterize today's siblings.

4. The example of Bharata's sacrifice in resolutely refusing the kingdom meant for Rama can offer a signal lesson for the many succession battles among children that break open after the death of a wealthy parent – and sometimes even before the death.

Inspiration, not imitation

At this point, we may object, "If we sacrifice like this in today's self-centered culture, we will be exploited." That's possible – and that's why the Ramayana tradition offers the examples of its protagonists not for imitation, but for inspiration: not for duplication of the particulars of their sacrifices, but for appreciation of the principle of sacrifice. As our relationships and interactions occur in real life, we need to consider the various contexts and their implications before we decide how to apply the spirit of sacrifice in our lives.

Lest we feel that the spirit of sacrifice is entirely inapplicable today, we need to look no further than popular team sports like cricket or soccer which throws up both jarring incidents when a self-seeking player chases after a personal milestone at the cost of the team's success and uplifting instances when a sacrificing player puts aside individual glory for the sake of the team's victory. If sacrifice plays a valuable, even critical, role in a relatively frivolous activity like team-sports, then how much more indispensable will be its role in real life relationships which are also like teams, but teams that last much longer and mean much more to us?

Shades of black

The Ramayana complements these examples of heroic selflessness with examples of tragic selfishness and its unfortunate consequences. Significantly, it demonstrates these ramifications of selfishness through characters with varying shades of blackness:

1. At the pitch dark end of the spectrum is the epitome of ungodliness, the demon-king Ravana, who due to his selfish lust, commits innumerable atrocities and finally meets his nemesis when his evil eye extends to Sita, the goddess of fortune.

2. Toward the middle of the spectrum is the monkey-king Vali, who lets himself be misled by a hasty and nasty misjudgment about his brother Sugriva's mentality and so selfishly dispossesses the latter of home, wealth and family, and eventually meets his own end in a heart-

rending fratricidal showdown.

3.   At the bright end of the spectrum is the queen Kaikeyi, whose temporary spell of selfishness perverts her from her normal kindness, gentleness and wisdom to an uncharacteristic cruelty, harshness and folly that causes agony to her family members, brings about the anguished death of her husband and subjects her to a lifelong regret for her insane self-obsession.

Thus, the Ramayana by illustrating its caveats about selfishness not just through outright ungodly characters but also through godly persons who succumb temporarily to selfishness inspires all of us to keep up our guard against selfishness and thereby prevent it from sabotaging our relationships.

Redefining the "we"

If this message of sacrifice as a means to deep fulfilling human relationships was all that the Ramayana offered to the world today, then that message in and of itself would be valuable. But the Ramayana's gifts are much greater and deeper.

The central hero of the Ramayana is not a human being, but the Supreme Being. Rama is an incarnation of the Supreme Lord playing the role of a human being. So the bonds of all the associates of Rama with him are examples of the human-divine relationship that is far more lasting than the best human-human relationship. All human-human relationships, even if fulfilling, are ultimately distressing due to the inevitability of rupture at death. But the human-divine relationship, when understood as a spiritual relationship between the eternal soul and the eternal Supreme, is eternal – and eternally fulfilling.

The Supreme Lord possesses fully and forever the six opulences – beauty, wisdom, strength, wealth, fame and renunciation – whose fractional and fleeting presence in worldly people attracts our heart to them. Lord Krishna indicates that the attractive features that worldly people possess ultimately originate from him when he states in the Bhagavad-gita (10.41), "Know that all beautiful, opulent and glorious creations spring from but a spark of my splendor." Just as the complete fire can provide far greater warmth than a tiny spark, the Supreme Lord can provide far greater warmth of love for our hearts than any worldly person.

In fact, the Lord descends as his various avataras to offer us this supreme warmth and ultimate fulfillment. The Bhagavad-gita (4.9) indicates that when we understand the true transcendental nature of the Lord's pastimes – the incredible loving exchanges between the Lord and his devotees that comprise their heart, then the desire to have a similar loving relationship gets kindled in our heart and that desire when fully developed helps us attain the Lord's eternal abode, where we eternally rejoice in love with him.

But developing our relationship with the Lord, like developing any other relationship, requires commitment and sacrifice. If we miss this essential point, then we end up conflating authentic spiritual life with the inanity of ritual religiosity or the "feel-good" sentimentality of new-age spirituality or any other similar form of shallow or shadow spirituality. The Ramayana conveys the necessity and the glory of sacrifice in the service of God through its refreshing portraits of extraordinary – and ordinary persons – who achieved deep devotional relationships with the Lord by activating their individual spirit of sacrifice.

Present-day reenactments of Ramayana principles

Srila Prabhupada embodied an unprecedented and unparalleled example of the same spirit of sacrifice in our times, when he at the advanced age of 69 went singlehandedly across the ocean to fulfill the mission of the Lord to share spiritual wisdom with the world. Thus he demonstrated how Hanuman's example of leaping to Lanka in service of Lord Rama can be followed today. Just as Hanuman searched zealously to find Sita in a Lanka that was densely populated with ungodly elements, Srila Prabhupada searched industriously for spiritually inclined individuals in a world that was densely populated with ungodly materialistic crowds.

The advanced age of Srila Prabhupada and the logical improbability of the success of his mission are evocative of the sacrifice of Jatayu, the aged bird who fought gallantly and became a martyr while trying to stop Ravana from abducting Sita. Srila Prabhupada's mission was as imposing and impossible as Jatayu's: to stop the rampaging advance of materialism and hedonism, symbolized by Ravana, from carrying sincere souls, symbolized by Sita, away from the devotional service of the Lord. But, by the miraculous mercy of the Lord, Srila Prabhupada was given the incredible potency by which he transformed mission impossible into mission unstoppable; he tirelessly circumnavigated the globe fourteen times, wrote nearly seventy books, established one hundred and eight temples and inspired millions of people to practice devotional service, not only stopping devotionally minded people from being carried away by materialistic allurements, but also redirecting materialistic people to become devotees.

Most of us may not be called upon to perform such herculean sacrifices, but we can sacrifice and contribute to the Lord's cause by rendering services according to our individual capacities, as did the monkeys to Lord Rama's cause. If we strive to serve the Lord sincerely, some of us may even discover hitherto unknown abilities within ourselves, as did Hanuman just before his stupendous leap to Lanka. Some of us may even become empowered to do extraordinary feats in the Lord's service, as was Hanuman.

Perhaps the most relevant example for us as spiritual seekers is that of Sita when separated from Lord Rama and held in captivity in Ravana's Lanka. All of us are also separated from the Lord of our hearts and are held in captivity in material existence which is the arena of Ravana-reminiscent materialism. Sita demonstrated her unfailing and unflinching devotion to Lord Rama by rigidly rejecting all the overtures of Ravana for ungodly indulgence and intensely absorbing herself in the remembrance of the Lord. We too can demonstrate our unflagging devotion to the Lord by firmly rejecting all the overtures for ungodly indulgence in meat-eating, gambling, intoxication and illicit sex, no matter how much the pressure from our social circle. We can gain strength to withstand such pressure by contemplating on the extremity of Sita's predicament. She was threatened with death if she refused to indulge – and yet she refused. Surely the pressure on us from our social circle is not that bad, then why should we give in to it? We can further strengthen ourselves by following in Sita's footsteps in attentively absorbing ourselves in the remembrance of the Lord – at least for the time of our mantra meditation.

When we understand these timeless devotional principles that underlie the stories of the Ramayana, then we no longer fall prey to the misconceptions that these stories are just outdated historical tales or mythological ethical parables; we recognize them to be authentic and dramatic demonstrations of eternal spiritual principles, principles that have inspired enterprising individuals to the highest human attainment throughout history and that beckon us to the same supreme adventure and accomplishment. Therein lies the ultimate, unfading relevance of the Ramayana. No wonder eminent literary historian A. A. MacDonnell noted about this timeless classic: "Probably no other work of world literature has produced so profound an influence in the life and thought of a people as the Ramayana."

To summarize, the Ramayana's perennial relevance lies in its power to inspire us to broaden our consciousness from "me" to "we" and to momentously expand the definition of "we" from the human-human paradigm to the human-divine paradigm.

Janmashtami meditation: Krishna is committed to our freedom. Are we?

Freedom. All of us want it. Some people strive for political freedom; others for cultural freedom. Almost everyone craves for financial freedom: the independence to spend as per desire without having to bother whether enough will be left to pay for necessary expenses.

The Supreme Freedom

Gita wisdom introduces us to a new kind of freedom: spiritual freedom. What is spiritual freedom? It is the freedom to delight in our own spiritually joyful nature, the freedom to be happy without depending on anything external for our happiness. As spiritual beings, we are *sat-cit-ananda*, eternal, enlightened and ecstatic. When we situate ourselves in our original spiritual nature, we become free to delight everlastingly in our loving relationship with Krishna, who is the supreme reservoir of all joy, love and beauty.

This spiritual freedom is the supreme freedom because, in a single stroke, it fulfills the ultimate purpose of all other freedoms: happiness. We seek political, cultural and financial freedoms because we feel that their absence blocks our pursuit of happiness. Unfortunately, our freedom struggles overlook the greatest freedom-blocker: materialism. When materialism brings us in its clutches, it perverts our sense of identity, making us imagine that we are our material bodies. This perversion makes us intrinsically, inescapably dependent on external material things for our happiness: "As I am a material being, I need material things to be happy. What can be more obvious than that?"

What is far less obvious is that this notion steals our freedom to be happy in ourselves, in our own internal devotional connection with Krishna.

Most of us are oblivious to this theft of our freedom. But Krishna isn't.

Krishna's Divine Dynamism

Krishna is unfailingly, unflinchingly committed to our freedom. He knows that we can reclaim our freedom only when we first get the knowledge of our spiritual identity and destiny; this knowledge makes us aware of the freedom we have lost. That's why Krishna himself shares spiritual knowledge and also sets up the system of *parampara* for the subsequent dissemination of that knowledge. The fourth chapter of the Bhagavad-gita (4.1-3) outlines how Krishna arranges all these resources by which we can reclaim our spiritual freedom.

Krishna's concern for our freedom is so great that it doesn't let him stay satisfied with making background arrangement; it impels him to spring into foreground involvement. Whenever he observes that materialism has started trumping spirituality (*dharmasya glanih*), he personally descends to the world to offer us a double reminder of what we are missing.

Firstly, he makes available once again the systematic philosophical knowledge that makes our spiritual potential transparently, temptingly reachable. In the Bhagavad-gita, he delineates the path of devotion that enables us to easily and efficaciously reclaim our spiritual freedom

Secondly, he demonstrates the reality, the sublimity, the beauty of this freedom by revealing his eternal pastimes with his devotees. These celebrations of unending love show how our longings for freedom that we are mistakenly striving to fulfill at the material level are naturally fulfillable at the spiritual level.

The Gentle-Yet-Grave Reminder

Janmashtami, the day when Krishna descends to our world, is a poignant reminder of how committed Krishna is to our freedom. This day offers us a precious opportunity to ponder on Krishna's total and tireless commitment to our freedom.

If we had but a fraction of the commitment to our spiritual freedom that he has, we would have been free from materialism a long time ago. However, we are so thoroughly deluded by materialistic propaganda that we mistake spirituality to be incarceration and materialism to be liberation.

Gita wisdom helps us realize how treacherous this misconception is. If we just ponder on the vast number of our unsatisfied material desires, on the sheer impossibility of fulfilling them and on the futility of the fleeting happiness that they offer even if we succeed in fulfilling them, we can recognize that materialism is the expressway to incarceration.

Krishna makes himself available in this age as his holy names. The Hare Krishna mahamantra is Krishna's sound manifestation that offers us all the blessings that his personal presence can offer. All we need to do is give up our lethargy in connecting with Krishna.

Janmashtami prods us out of our spiritual lethargy by the gentle yet grave question: Krishna is committed to our freedom. Are we?

The
Individual

The Worst of Ages, the Best of Ages

"Those who are actually advanced in knowledge are able to appreciate the essential value of this age of Kali. Such enlightened persons worship Kali-yuga because in this fallen age all perfection of life can easily be achieved by the performance of sankirtana."

- The Srimad Bhagavatam 11.5.36

The Vedic scriptures contain graphic negative descriptions of the present age of Kali as the darkest of all ages. Yet there are a few significant verses that glorify this age as the most spiritually opportune. Let's discuss what makes this age dark and what makes it bright.

Vedic wisdom explains that we are not bodies but are souls meant for the highest fulfillment of eternal loving relationship with Krishna in his supreme abode. As love is possible only when there is freedom, Krishna gives us free will and then guides us through *guru-sadhu-shastra* (spiritual master-saintly teachers-scriptures) how to best use our free will. But the very existence of free will requires the existence of an arena for the misuse of the free will. That arena is provided as the material world where we presently reside.

Two paths

That's why here we always have to choose between two essential paths: the path of virtue and the path of vice. The path of virtue helps us to ultimately return to Krishna, whereas the path of vice offers us innumerable alternatives to Krishna so that we can misuse our free will and play out our fantasies to enjoy separate from him.

All souls in all ages have to choose among these two paths. What makes the various ages different is that the number of people who choose vice increases from Satya Yuga down to Kali Yuga. Srila Prabhupada explains this downward slide through the four ages, "The cycle of Satya is characterized by virtue, wisdom and religion, there being practically no ignorance and vice, and the yuga lasts 1,728,000 years. In the Treta-yuga vice is introduced, and this yuga lasts 1,296,000 years. In the Dvapara-yuga there is an even greater decline in virtue and religion, vice increasing, and this yuga lasts 864,000 years. And finally in Kali-yuga (the yuga we have now been experiencing over the past 5,000 years) there is an abundance of strife, ignorance, irreligion and vice, true virtue being practically nonexistent, and this yuga lasts 432,000 years." Srila Prabhupada's carefully-worded description of Satya-yuga as having "practically no ignorance and vice" conveys the possibility of exceptions to the overall pattern of that age; occasionally, some demons might gain control briefly and propagate vice, but such periods are abnormal spikes of vice amidst a normal current of virtue. The spikes increase in frequency and duration with the passage of ages till the pattern is reversed in Kali-yuga: we have occasional spikes of virtue amidst a normal current of vice.

The Ethical Weather

We may wonder, "Do the moral patterns of an age determine the individual moral choices of the people of that age? Is this system fatalistic?"

No, declares Vedic wisdom. Let's understand how with an analogy. The four ages are like cosmic seasons. Just as the environmental weather changes from season to season in overall predictable patterns, the ethical weather changes from age to age in overall predictable patterns. In general, the moral characteristics of souls born in a particular age correlates with the ethical weather of that age. Thus, souls with a high moral sense are born in Satya-yuga and souls with a low moral sense are born in Kali-yuga. That's why vicious souls are exceptions in Satya-yuga and virtuous souls are exceptions in Kali-yuga.

Nonetheless, we always have our free will. Neither does the ethical weather of an age pre-program our moral choices, nor does it free us from karmic accountability for those choices. We can infer the enduring presence of free will from our own experience and introspection: we can observe that we consciously choose to do and not do certain things. Our inference is vindicated by, scriptural testimony. The Vedic scriptures declare that, to guide us to use our free will properly in every age, the Lord himself descends and also sends his representatives. Moreover, he also teaches a specific method of self-realization that is specially attuned to the ethical weather of that age. In this age, he comes as Lord Chaitanya Mahaprabhu and teaches the process of chanting the holy names, especially the Hare Krishna mahamantra. Due to this special redeeming arrangement, the ethical downslide in our age doesn't make us helplessly pre-programmed or justify our becoming morally degraded.

Making bad things worse

Continuing with the weather analogy, the rainy season brings a lot of rains, but that doesn't necessitate everyone getting drenched. People can use rain-protectors like umbrellas or rain coats and keep themselves dry. Similarly, amidst the rain of immorality that characterizes Kali-yuga, we can use the holy names that are a custom-made morality- protector for our times and keep ourselves virtuous.

Unfortunately, our society has not allowed matters to stay so simple. To understand how it has aggravated the existing mess, imagine that amidst heavy rains the society glamorizes those who open the roofs of their houses and get themselves thoroughly drenched. As if this were not bad enough, the intelligentsia rationalizes such self-wetting and the technology facilitates easy opening of the roofs. Then far, far more people will get wet than is necessary.

That is what is unfortunately happening in our age. Let's understand briefly how today the path of vice is socially glamorized, intellectually rationalized and technologically facilitated. For the sake of brevity, we will focus on the principal vice of lust, which the Bhagavad-gita (3.37) describes as the all-devouring sinful enemy of the world.

Socially glamorized: In the past ages, people who indulged in lust unrestrictedly or catered to lust professionally were not considered social models, as they frequently are nowadays. Men who are so enslaved by lust that they can do nothing better with their life than hunt for new sexual escapades were not seen as heroes, as happens today. Women who highlight and exhibit their sexuality by exposing their bodies were not portrayed as heroines, as is done these days. Public displays of sex are now called bold, not obscene. Because of such glamorization of lust, social pressure pushes people to aggravate their lust rather than subordinate it.

Intellectually rationalized: In the past ages, slavery to lust was recognized as a form of bondage that was harmful not just spiritually but also materially. But today that slavery is rationalized as "sexual freedom." Though this "freedom" results in most people staying perpetually agitated, tormented and entangled with lusty thoughts, the intellectual rationalization makes them think that they are "free." Nature has provided an inbuilt check on unrestricted sexual indulgence by biologically linking it with reproduction. Today the rationalization of population control is used to remove that check using contraception and abortion. Mothers are widely considered paragons of the noblest form of worldly love due to the tireless sacrifice they accept in taking care of their infant babies. Horrendously, today mothers are encouraged to become murderers of their babies by rationalizing abortion as "biological freedom" and condemning pregnancy as "biological slavery." Due to such rationalization, the normal intellectual defenses that protected people in the past from being tyrannized by lust are today in shambles.

Technologically facilitated: In the past, if lust overpowered people, the worst that they could usually do was go to a nearby red light area. But today if they become lusty, lewd images from all over the world are available just a few clicks away due, to the proliferation of internet porn. Exposure to such raunchy imagery fills the minds of people with mountains of filth. In all ages and in all parts of the world some people will inevitably be perverse. But consider what happens when the most depraved fantasies of such perverts are pooled together for easy access by anyone and everyone with a net connection. The perversity of perverts gets unlimitedly fueled, leading to despicable sexual crimes of the kind that we are seeing increasingly in society today: rapes, incest and pedophilia, for example. Majority of the people, though prone to lust, are usually not perverts. But when technology facilitates easy access to perversity, far more people than in the past become overrun by insatiable lust.

Our age is characterized by cultural glamorization, intellectual rationalization and technological facilitation of not just lust, but also greed and several other negative passions that impel people on the path of vice. That's why many more people succumb to much more vice than they would have otherwise. Consequently, they tragically bring upon themselves massive karmic implications and colossally increased bondage. Srila Prabhupada puts this insightfully, "Advancement of material civilization on the basis of sense gratification means increasing the duration of the material existence of a living entity."

A Devotional Culture

Despite these fearsome characteristics of Kali-yuga, there is still hope; there always is, because Krishna always loves all his children. No matter how wayward they become, he always provides them the way to return to him if they just desire to. As people are less spiritually inclined or qualified in this age than in the past, he makes the path of spiritual realization or yuga-dharma easier than in the past. The Srimad Bhagavatam (12.3.52) states, "Whatever result was obtained in Satya-yuga by meditating on Vishnu, in Treta-yuga by performing sacrifices, and in Dvapara-yuga by serving the Lord's lotus feet can be obtained in Kali-yuga simply by chanting the Hare Krishna maha-mantra."

The process of chanting is extremely easy when compared to the methods of self-realization for earlier ages: austere and prolonged yogic meditation, expensive and elaborate fire sacrifices, meticulous and majestic temple worship. At the same time, to sustain the practice of chanting throughout our life, we need a supportive culture. That's why the acharyas or spiritual teachers provide us a devotional culture in which the social, intellectual and technological trajectories are directed towards virtue, not vice as they are in the present culture. In this culture, those most devoted to Krishna are socially glorified; the logical and philosophical foundations of the supreme path of virtue – devotional service –

are systematically explained; and technological facilities are used to help us come closer to Krishna.

As practicing devotees, we need to adopt this culture as much as possible while practicing the process of chanting. Returning to our earlier analogy, if chanting is the umbrella, this culture is the overhead roof. Protecting oneself from heavy, stormy rains with an umbrella alone without any overhead roof is almost impossible – especially if the rains are prolonged. Similarly, to try to protect ourselves from the rains of immorality with the umbrella of chanting alone without the overhead roof of a devotional culture is almost impossible – especially because the rains of immorality are likely to continue lifelong. That's why the devotional culture is invaluable and irreplaceable.

As of now, this devotional culture is a small, culture in the mainstream materialistic culture. But the more we adopt it ourselves and share it with others, the more we can equip them to protect themselves from being slaughtered by the onslaughts of vice. Thus, we can become a part of a divine rescue operation that is prophesied to bring a mini-age of virtue amidst this age of vice. In the Brahma-vaivarta Purana, Lord Krishna informs mother Ganga about the presence of a virtuous mini-age in this vicious age, "For 10,000 years of Kali such devotees of mine will fill the whole planet." (Brahma-vaivarta Purana, Srikrishnajanmakanda, Uttara-arddhe, text 59).

Lord Chaitanya, the Kali-yuga incarnation of Krishna, inaugurated this golden age and Srila Prabhupada expanded its golden influence all over the world by his tireless outreach efforts. All of us have the fortune to receive and share this divine legacy and thereby become models and messengers of integrity amidst this age of perversity.

Tears of Sorrow, Tears of Gratitude: Seeing Krishna's Hand In the Tragic Deaths of Devotees

The Sometimes devotees meet with fatal accidents, as happened in June of last year when an air crash tragically killed eight dedicated members of the ISKCON Mumbai, Chowpatty, devotee congregation. As the community gathered to mourn the loss of their dear fellow devotees, one question arose repeatedly and insistently: "If Krishna is truly the protector of His devotees, then how can we make sense of such a ghastly accident?" This question resonates far beyond any particular event and relates to the overall pattern of Krishna's interactions with His devotees.

Tragedies like these are, no doubt, emotionally devastating, even for serious aspiring devotees who know that "we are not our material bodies." The path of bhakti doesn't ask us to suppress our emotions or reject them as illusory; it urges us to sublimate our emotions by connecting them with Krishna. Radhanatha Swami, the spiritual leader of the Chowpatty devotee community, poignantly expressed this insight with the gentle exhortation: "Let your every tear be a tear of gratitude to Krishna."

How can we possibly be grateful to Krishna in the face of great tragedy, especially when our fellow devotees are involved? Once we begin practicing devotional service to awaken our love for Krishna, everything that happens in our life is an opportunity to go deeper into that love. For that we should be grateful—even when opportunities come in the form of heartbreaking tragedies—because love for Krishna is indestructible, even by death. Let's understand this spiritual love better.

The Door Out of the Disaster Movie

All of us long to love and to be loved. Most of us seek love at the material level and thereby unwittingly become participants in a disaster movie.

Disaster movies generally show people caught in some natural calamity, trying heroically to save themselves and others from impending doom. Though disaster movies may be popular, not many of the people who like them would want to find themselves in an actual disaster; there's no guarantee of a fairy-tale ending. Even fewer are the people who realize that all of us face a real-life disaster that's unfolding before our eyes. The name of this all-consuming disaster is the relentless approach of death: A hundred percent of the people reading this article will be wiped out a hundred years from today.

Despite this hundred-percent casualty rate, most of us don't feel that life is like a disaster movie. One reason is that the movie of life unfolds in slow motion, allowing us to forget the direction of its motion if we want to. And we fervently want to. Why? Because the reality of death is inconvenient and unpleasant for us. It ruins our hopes for success and glory in the material realm. So we want to forget it. And forget we do.

But even if we forget it, the disaster movie is real. And we are not spectators. We are actors who dream of being victors but end up being victims.

This is our unfortunate fate as long as we seek love in the material realm. Bhakti shows us a way out of this doomed fate by connecting us with an eternal object for our love: Krishna. This connection doesn't stop the disaster of death, but enables us to come out of its path. To understand how, we need to review the philosophical fundamentals taught in the Bhagavad-gita.

Resolving Our Essential Dilemma

The Gita (2.11–30) informs us that we as eternal souls can't even be touched, let alone destroyed, by anything material—even death. The Gita (18.65–66) further reveals how Krishna offers us a standing invitation to a life of eternal love, a life outside the disaster-prone area of material existence. All we need to do is redirect our love towards Him.

When we start redirecting our love devotionally, Krishna expertly starts orchestrating our life and thereby providing us opportunities to increase our love for Him. Frequently, Krishna's orchestration provides us increased means to practice devotional service. However, the world simultaneously allures us with promises of material pleasure and distracts us from using these devotional opportunities. This underscores our essential dilemma as aspiring devotees practicing spiritual life in material existence: We need to act on both the spiritual and the material levels. At the spiritual level, we try to increase our love for Krishna by remembering Him internally and serving Him externally. At the material level, we act to use the material in service of the spiritual. Nonetheless, the material always has the potential to tempt us and mislead us away from Krishna. Whatever attachments we have to the material are hazardous distractions on our spiritual journey. Throughout our lives we struggle to protect ourselves from these allurements. Krishna helps us in our struggle by periodically showing us the insubstantiality of the material through the distress and disaster that characterize material existence.

Krishna-bhakti may or may not change the way material nature acts, but it definitely changes the way those actions of material nature affect us. So, although material nature may take its normal distressing course and cause tragedies even in the lives of devotees, the effect of such tragedies on devotees is different from that on nondevotees.

For those who have lived in forgetfulness of Him, Krishna as death comes to take away everything; as naked souls they have to go to the next life with nothing but the burden of their karma. For those who have been cultivating devotion, however, Krishna as death takes away whatever may have caused distraction from the treasure of bhakti.

This in fact is the vision with which Vyasadeva consoles Yudhißthira Maharaja, who was grieving the death of Abhimanyu, his young nephew, in the Kurukshetra war.

In the Mahabharata, Vyasadeva says, "No enjoyment in this world would be able to entice Abhimanyu away from where he has now gone, O King. He shines like a god in a splendid new body. We should grieve for those still living rather than for those who have attained such an end."

Thus, for devotees death is a transition that takes them from the arena of distraction to the arena beyond distraction or at least an arena closer to Krishna. To our finite material vision it may appear that this transition takes place gracefully for some devotees; they may depart surrounded by other devotees chanting and praying for them. And, to our finite material vision, it may also appear that this transition happens in a dreadful way for other devotees; they may depart in a tragic airplane crash, or in some other shocking way. But our finite material vision doesn't show us how Krishna is lovingly and expertly doing whatever it takes to clear off the residual distractions of those devotees and enable them to come closer to Him, undistracted.

The Vision of Faith

Of course, all of us have our own individual material distractions to remove, and Krishna knows much better than us the best ways to increase our devotional focus. That's why—though we may not know why things happen in a particular way, or where exactly someone will go after death—we can be sure about the safety of those who place themselves in Krishna's hands, for His are the safest of all hands. So we can be assured in our faith that Krishna has guided, even escorted, our departed devotee-friends to a level where they can focus primarily, or even exclusively, on their greatest treasure of devotion.

Srila Prabhupada urges us to adopt this vision of faith in his purport to Srimad-Bhagavatam 3.16.37, after discussing how throughout history various exalted devotees have severely suffered: "Seeing all these reverses affect devotees, one should not be disturbed; one should simply understand that in these matters there must be some plan of the Supreme Personality of Godhead. The Bhagavatam's conclusion is that a devotee is never disturbed by such reverses. He accepts even reverse conditions as the grace of the Lord. One who continues to serve the Lord even in reverse conditions is assured that he will go back to Godhead, back to the Vaikuntha planets."

It is natural that we agonize over the sudden loss of the company of our fellow-devotees, and it is natural that we shed tears of sorrow. At the same time, death reminds us that we have been gifted with a treasure that survives, even trumps, death and that we need to urgently enrich our hearts with that treasure before it is too late. We feel grateful to Krishna for having given us that treasure, for having connected us with devotees who by their living, and especially by their leaving, have increased our appreciation of the value of that treasure.

Thus does the sudden death of our fellow devotees cause us to shed tears of both sorrow and gratitude: sorrow because death has ended our connection with them in this world, and gratitude because Krishna has given us the opportunity to connect with Him and His family of loving devotees at a level that death can never bring to an end.

When Cancer Became a Blessing

(The gist of this article was told by Surapriya Mataji to her husband. He told that gist to Chaitanya Charan das, who integrated it with other relevant researched information to write this article.)

On August 18, 2002, my life took a fateful turn. A persistent leg-pain was diagnosed as being caused by malignant terminal breast cancer that had spread all over the body.

Till then my life had been, more or less, similar to that of most Indian Hindu housewives. I had been born and brought up in Maharashtra, a province in Western India, in a cultured and pious family and had married a respectable school teacher, Bhagavan Malwadkar, who went on to become the principal of his school. All our three sons became well-educated young men, with bright careers in front of them.

Then Lord Krishna entered my life. Two of my sons - Siddhanath and Santosh - met devotees of the ISKCON Youth Forum, Pune, in the middle of 1997 and, being inspired by their association, they took to the practice of Krishna consciousness enthusiastically. I was somewhat taken aback by their sudden transformation, but after I met Gaursundar Prabhu, the devotee who had preached to them, I was also attracted by his disarming simplicity and profound wisdom. My husband and I invited him to start a weekly Bhagavad-gita program at our house in Kothrud, one of the main suburbs of Pune and he agreed. As the weeks passed by, I was drawn more and more towards Krishna consciousness.

In the middle of 2000, both my devotee sons decided to renounce their promising careers to join ISKCON full-time to become brahmacaris (celibate preachers). I was aghast; all the dreams that I had cherished since their birth about their glorious future lay shattered. But I continued my devotional practices and gradually came to accept this as the inconceivable sweet will of the Lord. Meanwhile I suffered periods of poor health, but nothing seemed to be seriously wrong - till the day of that devastating diagnosis.

Within days of the diagnosis I was operated, but it was a lost cause. The cancer was so widespread, doctors told my family members, that treatment could at best delay the inevitable by a few months. Not only was the disease itself very painful, but the treatment brought its own pains with it and there was little chance that it would succeed. As the horrifying reality of my plight sank into me, I sensed that the pain, which was already excruciating, would keep worsening till the moment death took its final toll. I felt that it would be far easier to end my life myself right away than to try to endure the pain in an agonizing wait for an uncertain yet imminent death.

SPIRITUAL SOLACE

My sons, who had by now become initiated, (Siddhnath had become Sankirtananand das and Santosh had become Sundarvar das) were alarmed when I revealed my thoughts to them. In gentle yet firm words, they told me that suicide would not solve my problems; rather it would aggravate them. They explained how all suffering came upon one due to one's own past karma and could not be avoided by any artificial means. They cautioned me that my trying to escape my destined suffering through suicide would only postpone the suffering to my next life and that the reaction to the sinful act of destroying one's own body by suicide would add to that future suffering. It was better, they told me, to take shelter of Lord Krishna through devotional service, tolerate the suffering seeing it as His mercy, become purified and return back home, back to Godhead, never to take birth again in this world of suffering. They reassured me that prayerful remembrance of the Lord would provide me relief from my pain even in this life. I was stunned to hear such profound philosophy from my young sons, whom, just around two decades ago, I had nourished with my own breast milk. But soon the truth and the wisdom in their words entered my heart and I became filled with new hope. I resolved to spend the rest of my life cultivating devotional remembrance of Lord Krishna.

The doctors told me that I had around seven months left. I started thinking of King Parikshit, who had only seven days to prepare for his death. He had gone to the banks of the Ganges, heard Srimad Bhagavatam continuously for those seven days and had perfected his life. I decided to follow in his footsteps. I told my husband that I wanted to spend the last days of my life in the ISKCON temple at Pune. The Temple President, Radheshyam Prabhu, whom I had always revered as a very compassionate saintly person, promptly agreed to provide us a room in the temple premises. I was moved by his kindness as I knew there was an acute space shortage in the temple; forty-three brahmacharis lived in three rooms! We immediately moved into the temple. As I started taking darshana daily, hearing the classes and kirtans and reading Srila Prabhupada's books, I discovered something amazing: fixing my consciousness on Krishna protected me from the unbearable pain my body was inflicting upon me.

For a short period, my health seemed to improve and my husband and I returned to our home due to the shortage of space in the temple. But as soon as I left the temple, my bodily pain became so excruciating that I felt like I was being pierced from within at a thousand places. No amount of painkillers helped, but as soon as I returned to the temple, my pain subsided. I realized again that it was Lord Krishna who was protecting me from my pain, not the medicines. I begged to Radheshyam Prabhu to please allow me to spend the brief remainder of my life in the temple and he graciously consented, despite the inconveniences that it would invariably cause him and the other devotees in the temple.

Since childhood I had heard about krishna-bhakti and I knew that devotion was incomplete without initiation from a bona fide spiritual master. I started praying intensely, "Dear Lord Krishna, please give me the shelter of a guru before I leave this body." On January 23, 2003 I underwent a major surgery. In the course of the operation, my breath stopped completely for several minutes. During those traumatic minutes, I realized my identity to be distinct from my body; I could see, from a vantage point above the operation theater, my frail body lying lifeless on the operation table. I saw the doctors and nurses running around, trying frantically to revive me. I do not know what happened thereafter, but I woke up to find myself inside my body again. After that out-of-body experience (OBE) I felt intuitively that Krishna had given me a fresh lease of life just so that I could get the shelter of a guru. And, sure enough, on April 4, 2003, His Holiness Radhanath Swami Maharaj, the spiritual master of both my devotee sons, accepted me as his disciple and gave me the name Surapriya devi dasi. I loved my new name, which meant "the maidservant of one who loves the sweet sound of Krishna's flute".

In retrospect when I look back at my life and the great spiritual transformation that has taken place in it over the last few months, I feel strongly that cancer has proved to be a blessing for me. Had it not been for this deadly disease, I would never have risen about ritualistic piety to heartfelt devotion; I would simply have grown old, got diseased and died and continued on aimlessly in the cycle of birth and death. I would never have got the great fortune of living in the Lord's temple and I would probably never have sought or received initiation. And certainly I would never have experienced the sweetness of helpless remembrance of Lord Krishna. I feel therefore that the Lord has blessed me by giving me cancer and by simultaneously giving me shelter through His devotees and mission.

Generally when a young son renounces the world to serve God, his parents in particular and people in general are shocked at, what they consider to be, irresponsibility and escapism. I was no exception to such sentiments. My anguish was, in fact, much greater because, not one, but two of my sons decided to forsake everything for the Lord's service. But now on the verge of death, when the futility of all material achievements stands exposed before me and when the inestimable value of devotional service is dawning upon me, I realize how wise my sons were in dedicating their life to the service of the Lord in the prime of their youth.

During my sickness, my two devotee sons carefully attended to my needs, arranging for me to come and stay in the temple with them, cooking for me, accompanying me to the hospital and taking turns in serving me. Whenever I was in pain or distress, they were always there by my side to support and encourage me. They thus did all that a faithful son can be expected to do for his mother. But over and above caring for my body, they cared for the real me - my soul. They provided me with the spiritual knowledge and devotional practices, which saved me from unbearable bodily pain and brought me indescribable inner happiness. I therefore feel that what they have done for me is far more than what an ordinary son can ever do for his mother. I feel proud that they were so intelligent that they took to devotional service even before me. It is sometimes said that the child is the father of the man. In my case, the sons have become the spiritual guides of their mother. And lastly I feel profound gratitude to Srila Prabhupada, his followers and his mission, ISKCON, for having provided me with the shelter of Lord Krishna's lotus feet in my last days, when I so desperately needed it. It is only due to their grace that cancer has been transformed from a curse into a blessing for me.

* * * * * * *

Surapriya devi dasi passed away on June 13, 2003 at 3:15 am within the premises of Sri Sri Radha Kunjabihari temple, ISKCON, Pune. At that time, a CD player was playing a recording of Srila Prabhupada singing the Hare Krishna maha-mantra and her youngest son Sundarvar das was chanting on his beads next to her. Before losing consciousness the previous night, she repeatedly chanted the name of Srila Prabhupada and said that she very distinctly felt his presence in the room at that time, something which she had felt dimly on several occasions earlier. A few hours before her departure, her husband told her that his presence next to her would distract her from thinking of Lord Krishna at the time of death and that he would therefore go to a nearby relative's house for the night. She readily agreed.

During her last days, her relatives said that they saw no fear of death in her; rather they felt a divine peace pervade her being progressively. Even the doctors treating her commented that they had never seen a bone cancer patient so peaceful amidst so much pain. (Cancer spread through the bones is known to be extremely painful) She also requested her husband that, after her death, he should take to the vanaprastha (retired) order of life and dedicate his life to the service of Lord Krishna in ISKCON.

At the time of her initiation, Surapriya devi dasi wrote in her initiation form that she would like to preach Krishna consciousness. Devotees were surprised as to how she could possibly preach, being in such a precarious physical condition. She would fervently request every relative who came to see her to start chanting at least one round of the Hare Krishna maha-mantra. Most of her relatives, being moved by her earnest concern for their spiritual well-being despite being herself on her deathbed, started chanting at once.

Moreover Lord Krishna fulfilled His devotee's pure desire in a very special way. June 13 and 14 happened to be the dates of a spiritual youth camp at the Pune temple for over hundred and fifty devotee youths from all over India. By arranging for her death on the first day of this camp, Krishna gave all these youths a timely reminder of the harsh reality of death, a reality that most modern society tried to hide and ignore. Through her shining example, they also realized the necessity of accepting the saving grace of devotional service. Surapriya devi dasi thus preached the glory of devotional service through the way she accepted death. Krishna also glorified Surapriya devi dasi for her sincere devotion by arranging to have multitudes of devotees chanting to create an auspicious atmosphere at the time of her departure from her body.

Acknowledgements

The articles in this book have evolved gradually through my discussions with many learned and mature devotees.

HG Radheshyam Prabhu, my spiritual mentor and publisher, nurtured, shaped and directed my spiritual inquisitiveness right from the formative days in devotional service.

HH Bhakti Rasamrita Maharaj, my fatherly spiritual mentor, has guided and encouraged me to refine my study, writing and assimilation of Krishna consciousness.

His Holiness Radhanath Maharaj, my exalted spiritual master, provides unending inspiration by his words and actions in expertly presenting an ancient tradition to challenging contemporary audiences.

His Holiness Jayadvaita Maharaj, my writing-guru, has blessed me by reviewing many of my articles. By explaining the skills and the subtleties of the writing craft, he keeps prodding me onwards in the quest to become a better writer in the service of Krishna and Srila Prabhupada.

Many of these articles have been published in Back to Godhead. Those articles have benefitted immensely from the careful reviews of all the editors, Drutakarma Prabhu, Satyaraja Prabhu, Urmila Mataji and Vishakha Mataji and also the meticulous final editing of Nagaraja Prabhu. The articles that were published in Back to Godhead India have also been enriched by the inputs of Acyuta Prabhu. Working with all of them has not only improved the articles, but has also been among the most enriching and relishable experiences of my life.

Manish Vithalani Prabhu is an ever-available friend whose inputs have shaped many of these articles from conceptualization to actualization.

Madhusudan Vishnu Prabhu, ever the creative graphics expert, made the cover design. Hari Parayana Prabhu's thoughtful editorial inputs improved the books significantly. Avatari Chaitanya Prabhu also offered valuable suggestions.

Arjuna Sarthi Prabhu did the layout promptly and competently.

Trivikrama Prabhu helped with proofreading. Many others including Siddhartha Prabhu helped in various ways.

My heartfelt thanks to them all.

Chaitanya Charan Das

Books Published by VOICE

Essence of Bhagavad-gita (EBG) series:

- EBG Course-1: 'Spritual Scientist'
- EBG Course-2: 'Positive Thinker'
- EBG Course-3: 'Self Manager'
- EBG Course-4: 'Proactive Leader'
- EBG Course-5: 'Personality Development'
- EBG Vol -1 of 2 (Marathi)
- EBG Vol -1 of 2 (Hindi)

Spirituality for the Modern Youth series

- Discover Yourself
- Your Best Friend
- Your Secret Journey
- Victory Over Death
- Yoga of Love

Pocket Books

- How to Harness Mind Power?
- Practical Tips to Mind Control
- Can I Live Forever?
- Do We Live More Than Once?
- Misdirected Love
- E.N.E.R.G.Y- Your sutra for Positive Thinking
- Why do we need a T.E.M.P.L.E?

Other Books

- Youth Preaching Manual
- Bhagavad-gita 7 Day Course
- Values
- Frequently Un-Answered Questions
- Spiritual Scientist Vol I and II (Selected Newspaper articles)

- Science and Spirituality
- Idol Worship or Ideal Worship? (Questions & Answers)
- Oh My God! (Re-answering the Questions)
- My Little Bhakti Companion (Questions & Answers)

Children's Books:
- My First Krishna Book
- Getting to Know Krishna
- More About Krishna
- Deovtees of Krishna
- Wonderful Krishna
- Krishna's Childhood Pastimes
- Janmashtami
- Krishna Colors

Bring out the LEADER in you series

These books will be suitable for college students as well as corporates. The first book in this series has been published and the remaining will be released in the near future.

1. Stress Management
2. Time Management
3. Art of Self Management
4. Power of Habits
5. Secret of Concentration
6. Mind Your Mind
7. Positive Mental Attitude
8. Team Playing & Winning Trust of Others
9. Overcoming Inferiority Complex
10. Constructive Criticism – How to Give It or Take It?
11. Fate and Free Will
12. Karma – The Law of Infallible Justice

***

To read the author's daily meditations on the Bhagavad-gita, *Gita-daily,* and his weekly articles, you can register for daily feeds on his site www.thespiritualscientist.com. You can also ask him questions on his site.

***

69405063R00080

Made in the USA
Columbia, SC
21 April 2017